Endorsen

"I felt admiration, astonishment, and mystification about your brain all at the same time, many times. How can thoughts and knowledge co-exist with a lack of words? And now you are writing this book and writing it so powerfully.... I had five hours of sleep last night, and I am reading your book at eleven tonight – I can't stop."

– Irene Rinn, social worker and author

"I continue to be excited about the writing you are doing on your experience with the stroke.... I can't stop.... It's excellent!... It's even better than I imagined it could be."

– Jean Replinger, Minnesota Southwest State University,
Professor Emeritus, educator

"First of all, let me congratulate you on a fine piece of writing. Your present tense, stream of consciousness interiorization of your experience brims with that sense of the strange, confusing and awesome that you surely endured."

– Joe Paddock, author, poet,
oral historian, and environmental writer

"This is an elegant piece of writing! I am honored to be mentioned in the book."

– John Arnold, MD, retired

Aphasia, without speech:
A loss of the ability to use or understand words
as the result of brain damage caused by stroke,
injury or birth defect.

CROSSING THE VOID

My Aphasic Journey

Learning English the Second Time Around

Carol Cline Schultz

Chuckanut Enterprises, LLC

Crossing the Void: My Aphasic Journey
Copyright © 2010 by Carol Cline Schultz

Published by
Chuckanut Enterprises, LLC, PO Box 4193, Bellingham, WA 98227.
www.CrossingTheVoid.com

This is a non-fiction work. All places and people are real. The names of some people have been changed. The information concerning medical issues and aphasia recovery contained in this book is not meant to supplant professional counsel. Medical and recovery decisions require professional supervision. Neither the author nor the publisher is liable or responsible for any loss, injury, or damage allegedly arising from any information or suggestion in this book.

ISBN-13: 978-1-4505-0120-0
Library of Congress Control Number: 2010907882

Cover illustration: Vivid Brain © Kts | Dreamstime.com
Cover design and prepress: Kate Weisel (weiselcreative.com)

Printed in the United States of America

Dedication

Dedicated to my husband, Frank, for his steadfastness and long-suffering patience through the two times he lost me; first to the stroke, and then during the writing of this book. Now, at last, he can have his wife back.

Contents

Dedication v

Words Before ix

Brain MRI Image x

Part One: Entering the Void 1

Part Two: St. Joseph Hospital 25

Part Three: Going Home 61

Part Four: Running the Medical Gauntlet 79

Part Five: Quest for Words 107

Part Six: The Language of Numbers 133

Part Seven: Where Does Learning Go When It Can't Go
                 Where It's Been? 141

                 Brain Language Pathways Diagram 145

Part Eight: How Long Did It Take You? 147

Glossary 185

Appendix A: Insights for Advocates 193

Appendix B: Tim's Consonant Key 197

Appendix C: Tim's Consonant Sound Key Summarized 199

Appendix D: McCrackens' *Spelling Through Phonics* –
                 Sample Work 201

Appendix E: The Language of Numbers Key 203

Appendix F: Finding the Forty Sounds 205

Appendix G: Working with Forty Sounds 207

Appendix H: Information Contacts 209

Acknowledgements 211

About the Author 213

Words Before

This is a true story. I wrote it after a stroke took my words leaving me unable to speak, read and write – and after I learned how to teach myself those skills again.

Called aphasia, *without speech,* this condition presents itself to the victim as an inability to say words and, sometimes, the inability to understand the spoken word. Aphasia is due to brain damage caused by stroke, injury or birth defect.

Aphasia comes with difficult to answer questions. For example, what is it like inside the aphasic mind? How does one learn to speak, read and write when an impaired brain prevents landing spots for that learning? Where does learning go when it cannot go where it has been?

To realistically portray the early aphasic experience, and answer its questions, **Crossing the Void** should have been told as it was then. Silently, on empty pages ... wordlessly. But how could you have understood, and how could I have written ... without words?

Even as I begin to write, I teeter on the brink between two worlds. The one, of not being able to find the words I need, and the other, of almost always being able to find them. It is almost too soon to be writing, as words still come at a premium. It is not easy, this chore ... but manageable.

The Void

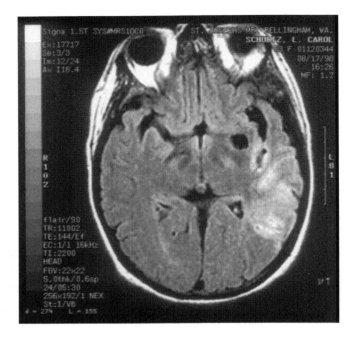

Magnetic resonance imaging (MRI) of the author's brain the day after her stroke. Viewed as if looking up from below, the right side of the image is the left side of the brain. The infarct is seen as the clouded area on the right side of the image.

Part One

Entering the Void

There's a land where the mountains are nameless,
And the rivers all run God knows where ...

There's a land—oh, it beckons and beckons,
And I want to go back—and I will.

—Robert Service, *The Spell of the Yukon*

Mysterious, compelling, the Yukon had called to us, too, as it had beckoned Robert Service. My husband and I are returning from our second canoe trip in the Yukon. As outdoor enthusiasts and owners of a specialty sporting goods store, we had first paddled the Yukon River from Whitehorse following the route of the gold rushers to Carmacks two years ago. Now we have paddled down the Teslin and Yukon Rivers from Johnson's Crossing to Carmacks with my sister, Betty Ann, and our friend, Randy.

I had been eager to go back to the Yukon. But this time it has not been the same. Usually on a trip like this, even at 53 years old, I feel better and better and stronger and stronger as the days go on. This time, I have not. Always short of breath with an elevated pulse, no energy, no strength. I am not definably sick, but neither am I well.

This morning in Whitehorse, we put Betty Ann on a plane to Boston, Massachusetts. Frank, Randy and I plan to take three or four more days to drive down the Alaska Highway to our home in Bellingham, Washington. Tonight, we have made camp in a campground just a few miles south of brilliantly aqua-green Muncho Lake in northern British Columbia.

The campground is in a partially cleared area with primitive camp-sites located around a loop road through the trees. The store/gas station/restaurant is by the highway and is noteworthy for having a nice, well worn bathhouse with a shower that has lots of hot water – a welcome switch from the metered showers in most of the tourist showers in the Yukon. After settling in, we sack out in our tent while Randy starts snoring in his.

The nightmare does not pass

I am restless in a strange sleep. In a quandary how to make myself quiet. I start with my knees propped up to lessen the back pain that's been with me this trip. When lying on my back brings no relief, I lie on the left side until my arm goes to sleep. Then I switch to the right side until the other arm goes to sleep. Thick mucus accumulates. My mouth wants to clear it. Cannot clear it.

In my sleep, I am in a bad dream. I am half asleep and half awake. My being half asleep hears Nature calling me to go outside the tent into a raging storm. My being half awake knows there is no storm outside the tent. It is calm outside. The storm is in me.

The conflict between them leaves me confused. It would be nice to go to the bathroom, but I do not want to deal with a storm's turmoil. I do not want to go outside. To get dressed. To fight the rain, the cold, the wind. Hold it. Postpone it. This storm will pass. This nightmare will pass. Sleep.

The nightmare does not pass. Something is not right. Can I find a better position? I thrash. My arm is asleep. My throat is stuck to itself. I need to move. I want the turmoil to go away. Want to sleep. Want peace. The raging storm will not leave my head. Through it, I hear Frank's voice: "Carol, are you all right?"

Why is he bothering me? I respond by muttering to him. My head does not want to wake up. *How much time passes?*

Frank is insistent, "Carol, are you okay?"

Did he not hear me? I am so tired. Again, I mutter to him.

I struggle to find peace. Frank rustles. I think he is getting up to go to the bathroom. I should go too. Then maybe I can find rest.

"Carol, what's the matter with you?" he demands.

Frank:
I was awakened about two a.m. by Carol thrashing around on her side of the tent. We were sleeping under, not in, our sleeping bags. I asked her several times what the matter was but she didn't respond, just kept on moving around. I turned on my headlight and asked, "Carol, are you all right?"

I make my mind open its eyes and see him sitting beside me with his headlamp beam focused on me. *Why is he looking at me?* He never turns his flashlight on to look at me. What is the matter?

My head slowly and deliberately thinks out my condition. I want to answer. I think out the thoughts carefully. My throat attempts to clear its thickness. I speak. The sounds are gibberish.

Frank:
She was lying there with a blank, vacant stare on her face and emitting some faint, guttural grunts.

Have I had a stroke? Frank's father had a stroke some years earlier. Even without words for them, I recognize that my speechlessness is a symptom.

Frank is visibly alarmed. I see he wonders too. He pulls my sleeping bag aside to look at my right arm. I know what he is looking for. He knows loss of speech often includes right side paralysis. I know that too. My right arm is dead.

I have had a stroke.

I pull my right arm up with my left and place it over my chest. Frank covers me with my sleeping bag. He says, "I'll take care of you. I'll find help."

Frank:
I alerted Randy that Carol had had a stroke, and we had to get her to help. We both dressed, and got Carol into the van, leaving our camp to take care of itself.

My head fights to think clearly. I want to stay awake. Murkiness threatens to erase clear thinking. I want to go back to sleep. Between being asleep and being awake I wonder. *Is this the beginning of the stroke or the end? Will I lose my right leg too? More? Where is this stroke going? Is it going to a nursing home? How will Frank manage?* Between sleep and wakefulness, I wait.

There are talking sounds in the dark. I think this will take a long time. Randy always takes a long time to get out of his tent in the morning. My body says *sleep*. I doze.

Frank crawls back through the tent door to sit by my side. I rouse but as in a dream. I am watching myself in a dream. The dream goes on. Frank talks to me. I listen. Try to make sense of what he says. It takes all my power. He lifts me up to a sitting position. Puts his arms around me. Holds me close. Prays. I do not understand what he says, but I know he prays to our God Jehovah. Frank needs strength beyond his own, and he is frightened. I need the strength too, but I am not frightened. With Jehovah, Frank will care for me.

Frank finds my clothes from the night before. He works the micro fleece pullover over my head, through my dead arm, and around my upper body. Feels good. He wants to know if my leg works. *Will I be able to help him?* My leg works. He pulls up my pants and fastens them for me. Socks. He dresses me as he would a baby. Frank is going to take me out of the tent. *Why?* My head wants to rest. My body does not want to crawl out of the tent. I hear sounds about how to get me out of the tent. Randy asks Frank if they will have to pull me out.

I do not want to crawl out of the tent. My back hurts. No words. Frank helps me up to the tent door. Puts on my boots. Folds my body through the tent opening. On each side Frank and Randy lift me out of the tent. Hold me up. I need two men to help me walk. My body has no strength. My head is mush.

I fight the mush. My head tries to work. Tries to make sense. I am resigned. I go.

Frank and Randy place me into the front passenger's seat. Frank covers me with my down sleeping bag. The down folds around me. My warmth meets it. It envelopes me, keeping out the night's cold. I rest from the exertion of moving from the tent.

Going for help

They leave the gear. Headlights flood the campground. Turn onto the perimeter road. The beams scan past the outhouse. Need to use the toilet. No words to ask. My body does not have the strength to gesture. One arm still hangs limp. Darkness passes the outhouse as we drive on.

They don't stop at the campground entrance. Frank drives onto the highway. He turns right. *Right?* Bellingham, where we live, is south. Should be turning left.

Frank:
The campground had no telephone. The lodge back at Muncho Lake would have one or there would be one at the ranger station nearby. I drove the winding road along the shore of Muncho Lake, trying to keep Carol conscious, trying to hold her upright in the car seat, crying, and praying out loud for help.

Dozing in and out of consciousness, I know where I am; I do not know where I am. I know this road but have no word for the name of this road. We continue north. I have no words to say it, but I know it. We are going away from home.

Where? It is a full yesterday's distance to the last big city. My mind knows no name for it now, but it will have a hospital. *Where are we going?* The air is tense as Frank and Randy trade urgent words. Ranger station? RCMP? Phone? I slump in the bucket seat that is always uncomfortable when I try to sleep in it. Quiet talk whispers through to me. It gently punctuates stress. Punctuates urgency.

The van rolls back and forth as it banks with each tight curve. It suggests we have come to Muncho Lake. I picture it in my head. The rock dips sharply to meet the water. The road follows a narrow cut bank, squeezed between the lake on the left and the rock wall on the right. My eyes open to see, but I am slumped too low. Too dark. Then I see the rock illuminated by the headlights. It is as I imagine. As I remember. My eyes close and rest while the road rocks me back and forth. Back and forth between the water and the rock.

The van slows. Turns. Comes to a halt. Headlights flood the front of a log lodge. We had been in the lobby before inquiring about the inn. The lodge is dark. Bang, bang, bang. Frank and Randy bang on the door; bang on the windows. I close my eyes while they rap. New voices sound. Lights come on the porch. Lights come on in the lobby. There is talk. I doze.

Frank:
We arrived in the parking lot of the High Peaks Lodge, a beautiful log building with plenty of lights but no night bell. I pounded on the door and window for several minutes. My hands were sore from pounding before someone inside turned on a light and asked what we wanted. I replied that we had a medical emergency; my wife had had a stroke and we needed medical help.

They opened the door, and we began the process of getting an ambulance from the BC Ambulance Service. As it turned out, in the 400 miles of the Alcan from Watson Lake to Fort Nelson, there was only one ambulance and it was at Toad River 75 miles away. Once the ambulance had been dispatched, I called our friend and neighbor, John Arnold, who is a physician, asking him if he could confirm my diagnosis of a CVA (cerebrovascular accident).

He said that he would walk right over to our house and had I called 911 yet? I explained that we were 1200 miles north of the border and I was trying to get Carol evacuated to medical help. John signed off saying that he would help set things up in Bellingham and at the hospital and would alert our son Tom to help coordinate the evacuation.

We made several calls to the RCMP (Royal Canadian Mounted Police) to try to get a medevac flight, but it turned out the ambulance was the only hope, and they showed up about 5 a.m. I asked if they had a paramedic on board. The driver allowed as how they didn't operate like that in Canada, but that they would take good care of us. Barry, the driver, and Trish, the attendant, were some of the most caring and gentle people I've ever run across.

I lie alone in the van. In my dozing, I think a long time passes. Frank comes to talk to me from time to time as the night passes. He tries to encourage me. His voice is earnest. He is taxed to the limit. He speaks of having talked with someone on the phone. From the way he speaks, I think that person is an authority and an intimate friend. Most of the talk does not find a place in my head. My head wants to think. Tries to think. It cannot. A thick blanket around my head muffles thinking.

How long is long? I sense I wait a long time before the ambulance comes. There is a man and a woman. Voices. They make talk. I do not. I have no voice. They talk about me. Clipboards. Paperwork. They are taking care of me. They check my blood pressure. They check my pulse. I am moved from the car seat to a litter. Placed in the ambulance.

It is cold when they take off my sleeping bag to transfer me to the ambulance. I want my sleeping bag. They cover me with a blanket. It is not as nice. Not as warm. I need warm.

The man and the woman are caring and gentle. They make comforting sounds. I understand some of the talk. Some of the talk, I do not. They tell me their names. I remember them by their compassion. By their careful actions. By the way the woman kindly places the pressure cuff around my arm. By the gentle way the man talks to me about the mask he will place over my face. He does not want me to be afraid. He carefully places the mask over my face.

Oxygen. My head has no word for it. But I know it is the part of the air my head needs.

Thinking without words

The man and the woman get ready to close up the ambulance. The woman sits next to me with a clipboard. The man moves to the driver's seat. Frank has been outside. The tail lights of our van and the ambulance meet in one brightness. Frank is stepping into the back of the ambulance. Crouching, he starts to pull the back doors closed to latch them. He pulls one and then the other. Before they close I see the canoes hanging over the back of the van. The stern lines dangle loosely. I want to tell Frank to tie them down.

Frank, fasten the lines. But thinking does not find words for my mouth.

I could show him how to fasten the lines. I see it. I feel it. My head senses the motion of running the line down through the ring on the hitch. I picture the motion of the trucker's hitch we use to secure the lines. I imagine throwing two twists. Pulling the main line through the loop to make a second. Threading the tail end through the loop. Pulling it tight. Securing it with a bow half hitch. Part of my head knows the way. I could do it myself if my arm could. But it is limp.

I rise to point toward the canoe lines. He motions me down. He reassures me. Randy will take the van back to the campground. He will stay with me. Frank latches the doors. I hope Randy will secure the lines.

Randy will go back to the campground. *Why? Shouldn't he follow us? What if we need the van?* I should talk with Frank about it. My head is thick. Cannot find the words through the fog. Very tired. I stretch out. Try to be comfortable. Try to be warm. Try to sleep. We return along the rolling road between the water and the rock. South.

The ambulance is a cold metal box. It is cold. The litter is cold. I am cold. Slowly the cold box warms as it lumbers down the road. At intervals the blood pressure cuff tightens on my arm. Then relaxes. The woman counts my pulse. The oxygen mask covers my face.

Frank:
On the drive, I tried to help reassure Carol and not get in the way; Barry remarked that if I heard the siren, I shouldn't worry about it – he was just getting caribou or moose off the road.

In my sleeping, needles are pricking my right arm. I reach to pull it up to my chest. I rub it. Knead it. Sensation is coming back. It works of its own accord. The oxygen is working. Frank notices the arm is moving. I keep moving my arm. I want to keep it. I need it. I am grateful. Will my words come back as easily? I breathe in the oxygen. I doze, waiting. Waiting for words to come back.

The cuff tightens and releases. The ambulance lumbers toward Toad River as day dawns. I see glimpses of light through the ambulance windows. My mind also sees glimpses of clarity as the blanket of fog lifts. The fog comes and goes as a mist. Swirling. Through the mist are periods of clearer thinking.

I think I can talk. I think the words will come. I try to tell Frank I am better. This stroke will not last long. He should not worry. I speak.

His reply is not relevant to my words. Frank is not encouraged.

Toad River

The ambulance rolls to a stop. The door opens. My eyes turn to look at this place. They call it Toad River. My mind hears the words but will not remember them, will not move the sounds to my lips. Through the open side door of the ambulance, I recognize the garage of a rustic gas station. We have been here before.

Frank bolts toward the door to find the toilet. Obviously, we both have the same pressing need. I am two opportunities behind needing to go to the toilet myself. I try to rise from the litter to go with him. Frank asks if I want to go to the bathroom. I nod. He says for me to wait. He will go first. Does he think my bladder has less urgency than his since I cannot speak? I hold it.

Frank gets back. I try to rise to take myself to the bathroom. Frank and the woman see I want to stand. I rise slowly and they help me sit by the litter. Remove the oxygen mask. One on each side they hold me to stand. We walk. My mind concentrates with each measured step. Unsteady. Uncertain. Slowly. Their support is welcome. It is a long few yards over the gravel pathway to the back of the building. We reach the door. The cracked concrete step up to the toilet room is as I remember. We have been here before on our trips up and down the road.

Propped up against the sink and balanced against the wall, I stand. My eyes watch both hands manipulate my clothing. My right hand works now. Sigh. It is gratifying. It is a simple matter-of-fact gratification. I have neither the mental energy nor the emotional stamina for enthusiasm.

Taking in the day void of words

Exhausted from the physical exertion going back and forth to the restroom, I sit down in the side door of the ambulance to rest.

I take in the day. Breathe it in deeply. Inhale its essence. It is daylight, but there is no sun. Early daylight in the August North announces itself long before the sun makes its presence. Diffused light bathes the earth in the warmth of a silky kiss. Soothing. Assuring. Hopeful. It is the promise of the sun to come.

I take in myself. If only I felt about myself as I felt about the day.

Instead, within me is a mellow emptiness pronounced by its lack of expressiveness. Empty, as the sun's absence from the early morning light – but where the light from the sun shows promise, there is no such hope for me. There is no reassuring kiss. My expressive sun is empty. Void of promise.

Tiredness takes over. It is time to stop thinking. Time to rest. Frank and the woman help me back to the litter. Put the oxygen mask back on my face. I stretch out. Relax. Let my body heal.

> **Frank:**
> The sun was coming up just about the time we got to Toad River, and a Bell Jet Ranger 206 was sitting right by the highway. Trish and I got Carol to the restroom for a necessary break, and then the paramedic on the helo packaged her into the litter. There was no place for me to ride along. It was 150 miles to the hospital at Fort Nelson, and I was on my own as far as getting there. Randy was back at the campground. I had no idea if he would even try to get to Fort Nelson that day.

Frank tells me a helicopter is on its way. We are going to the hospital at a familiar place name from the road map. I do not think we have been there. There will be help there.

There is talk. The helicopter is landing. The ambulance takes us to the helicopter pad. More talk. I want to see what is going on, but I am inside the ambulance and cannot see outside. Frank tells me it is a small helicopter. There will not be enough room for him. The attendant from the helicopter comes into the ambulance and speaks reassuringly to me.

He asks questions. I think very hard. I nod *yes* and shake my head *no*. I concentrate very hard. I try to say *yes* and *no*. He asks if I am frightened because my husband cannot go with me on the helicopter. I had not thought about whether I should be frightened. It was just the way things would be. I think about his question. I think *no*. I shake my head slowly and deliberately. *No*. Slowly and deliberately. Like my mind works.

I have no identity

Why did he ask? I am independent. I am used to taking care of myself. I am accustomed to managing in my husband's absence. Then I see.

This is not the usual absence. This is different. Without words I have no identity. I cannot tell anyone who I am, where I live, who my family is. I am being entrusted to strangers to go by helicopter to a place I do not know. And I cannot talk. *Should I be frightened?* I have to trust that someone has all the information about me on a piece of paper. I must trust that the piece of paper comes with me. Strangely, I am without distress. Without fear. I trust.

It is time to get into the helicopter. I picture myself walking up to the helicopter, stooping low under the whirling blades and jumping in like I did in Alaska in 1971. But this is an ordeal. The helicopter is missing half its bubble. The left side of the cockpit has no seats. I am moved with the ambulance litter to the helicopter pad. I am transferred to a litter that will fit inside the helicopter.

Frank stands beside me. His words say he wants me to think he is not worried. That I should not be worried. His face shows me that he is very worried. I worry more for him than for myself. Frank senses this is the moment of parting. He gives me a kiss. More lovingly and most reassuring, he fastens my fanny belt around my waist. There are words in my fanny belt. The words are my identity. The words will talk for me.

The men ready the litter to lift me up into the helicopter. They cover me with a blanket. They strap me down to the litter. The straps are tight. My legs are too tight. It makes my back hurt. The men fold the litter and lift me up into the helicopter. They place my feet near the front. They fasten the clear bubble over me. It surrounds me. I can see over my head. I can see to the front. Beside me. Below me on the left side. The pilot gets into his seat in the front by my feet. The attendant sits behind him next to my head. They put earphones on their heads. The attendant puts one on my head. We can hear and speak to one another. Speak?

Frank:
When the helo lifted off with Carol, I headed across the highway for a bit of breakfast before starting to hitch a ride. Trish looked at the trucks in the parking lot at the Toad River Lodge and said one big tanker truck belonged to a friend of hers named Ted.

Inside the restaurant, the air was thick with cigarette smoke from all the truckers at breakfast. Trish took me to a table with a lone trucker sitting by a cup of coffee and introduced me to

Ted. I asked him if he could take me to Fort Nelson when he left and he said, "Only if you'll have breakfast on me," thinking I was broke.

I gave big hugs to Barry and Trish, joined Ted for breakfast, and before long, we were climbing up into the cab of a big Kenworth semi and full trailer propane tanker. Ted was an open book as far as the territory we were driving through; he knew the names of all the rivers, where the best hunting and trapping was. He generally kept talking to keep my mind off Carol and our troubles.

The helicopter lifts off

The helicopter lifts off, slides forward, rises, pivots. With the gain in elevation, the morning sun rises, striking the bubble. Blinds me. The sun's heat soaks into my blanket. Soaks into myself. The lashed straps smother me with restraint. I am too hot. My back hurts. I squirm. The attendant sees my discomfort. Loosens the straps. I push down the blanket. I can raise my knees. He puts a blanket under my knees. I fall back against the pillow. Exhausted.

Eyes close. Body says rest. Rest my logy mind. No. We are in a helicopter. What portion of me wills my body to stay awake? Wills my dulled thinking to function a little longer? Something within me forces my eyes to open. My body rolls over. I crank my head over the edge of the litter.

It is worth the effort. It is beautiful. Such peace. I want to watch the view of the mountains. It is the same range we walked into from the road two years ago. We looked for sheep and goats. The attendant props me up so I can see better. The early morning sun glances obliquely to meet each peak. The mountains' highs and lows are accentuated by the deep contrasts of light and dark. Such a sense of well-being in spite of the fact that my head is not functioning well. I want Frank to see. He could tell me the geology. I resolve to come back with him. To come back again whether I talk or not. Talk or not? How will I express this desire? If I do not talk?

I watch. Barely able to keep my head up. I must not waste the scene. In the rocky areas above timberline and between snow patches, I watch for sheep and goats. Climbers. I see none. We are too high. The mountains are starting to move away. A bank of clouds is coming in. So tired. I roll back to the bed.

I wonder what time it is. I ask the attendant by pointing to the white stripe of flesh against the tan on my left wrist. I tap my finger. Tap. Tap. He asks if I am worried that my watch may be lost. My head shakes, *No*. Tap, tap, again. He asks if I want the time. I nod. He looks at his watch. He says the time. I do not understand. My hand takes his hand. My eyes look at his watch. The hands say 8:45.

I close my eyes. Try to sleep. I hear talking sounds come through the earphone. I think it is the airport control tower giving the pilot information. I think the earphone is not a very good one. The sounds are indistinct. Garbled. I doze through the garble.

Vaguely familiar words suggest we are landing in Fort Nelson. I wonder if we will land at the hospital. We seem to land somewhere else. The bubble comes off. There is another litter transfer. Another move to another ambulance. This time there are no questions about me. No checking up on me to see how I am doing. There are two men in the back of the ambulance with me. They do not talk to me. They talk to each other about their lives.

I listen very carefully. I try to make sense of the words they talk. The words get stuck between being out there and being in my head. *Are my ears plugged from the flight? Am I becoming deaf?* I think hard to make sense of this unawareness in my head. I swallow. My ears are not plugged. They are clear. My ears are not deaf. They hear. Then. Slowly. Awareness awakens. It is worse. This stroke. Worse than I thought. It is not the malfunctioning earphones. It is not the people talking indistinctly around me. The words are not garbled. My head garbles the words. Not only can I not talk words. Neither do I receive all of them. My brain does not understand my own language when spoken between others. My own language ... is a foreign language.

Fort Nelson

This is Fort Nelson in a real hospital in a real emergency room. The ambulance attendants transfer me to a gurney. The nurse is pleasant to me. She is not excited about me. She does the usual ER nurse things. My canoeing/traveling clothes come off. The typical hospital smock goes on.

The nurse offers me some water. I hesitate. I wonder. What did she say? She shows me the cup of water. I nod. I sip. She pulls it away before I can finish. She says why. I don't understand. I do not understand what she said. I do not understand why I cannot have more water.

Mostly I wait. I wait not understanding why I wait. Except I must wait for Frank to get here. The nurse checks to see if I need a blanket. She leaves. I wait.

The next time she comes in I ask for water. Do the words come out of my mouth? I think not. I gesture to suggest lifting a cup of water to my mouth. She asks if I want water. I nod. This time I drink the whole cup of water very quickly before she can take it away. I know I have been too long without water. Every cell in my body depends on water for its functioning. My brain must especially need it by this time.

A doctor comes. He examines me. He shines a flashlight in my eyes. He has me follow his fingers with my eyes. He looks in my mouth. He asks me to wiggle my tongue. He asks questions. I listen very carefully to understand his words. I try to really answer with words through my mouth. I think words come out. He accepts my words. Easy words. Like *Yes. No.* Have I had any illnesses? "No." Do I have any pain? I point to my back and my left shoulder and neck. He examines my arms and legs. He compares their strength. My right limbs are weak, but I'm pretty proud they function. He asks if I have had any paralysis. I do not have words to explain. But I know what he wants. I gesture, *this one.* I use my left arm to raise my right arm off the bed. Then I let my right arm fall limply to the bed. He seems to understand.

The doctor says, "I think you have had a TIA (transient ischemic attack). We will keep you here overnight. In the morning you will have recovered, and you will be ready to travel again."

That is good news. I have heard about TIA's before. Old people have them when their arteries get plugged up. They clear up within 24 hours. I will be able to talk in the morning. This is very good news! I can connect with Frank and Randy and resume our journey home. In two or three more days I will be back home and back to work.

The doctor leaves. The nurse puts me into a room. I wait. I wonder. I wonder where this stroke will go. I should keep trying to make my mouth work. If this is a TIA, words might start popping out of my mouth anytime. Mostly I wonder where Frank is. Has he found a ride? Is he still thumbing beside the road?

> **Frank:**
> Ted let me off on the main road, since his rig wouldn't get around the streets by the hospital. I walked up the hill to the hospital, checked in, and soon found Carol in a private room, looking pretty alert and relaxed.

It is a quiet Sunday. The hospital is quiet. It is small but modern. I think everyone in Fort Nelson must be very healthy. I seem to be the only patient in the hospital. There is no activity, no bustle. The hospital echoes as a cavern, as the echoes in my head. I hear talking sounds in the hallways. But I cannot understand them. I doze ... try to sleep to conserve my energy. Then through the haze of voices I hear Frank's name. *Is Frank here?*

The nurse comes to my room. She speaks to me. Frank is on the outskirts of Fort Nelson. He will be here soon. I wait. I listen. I hear Frank's voice in the hallway. Then he is beside me. I do not know how far it is from Toad River to Fort Nelson, but I expected Frank to take longer to get here. "How are you?" he says.

"Okay," I say. I say more, but Frank does not understand me. The words are gibberish.

Words do not find a landing spot

Frank goes on with his narrative about things that do not relate to what I wanted to say. He tells me his story. He is still out of breath from running up the hill to the hospital. His face shows a bead of sweat. His sweat smells like it is hot outside. It also carries the faint smell of stress and anxiety. His sweat smells like Frank.

It is a good story. I visualize it. My mind makes pictures from his words. His words do not find a place with the pictures he gives me. The words keep trying to go to the word place, but that spot is not accepting orders. My mind immediately forgets the words. I want to remember the words to repeat the story. But the words do not find a landing spot. I will have to ask Frank about it again later when I am able to talk words to him. Tomorrow the TIA will have resolved. I will have words tomorrow.

Frank:
She was able to speak almost normally, but every few words would be gibberish. Her arm seemed to work normally, but I was getting really worried about her speech. They had not used oxygen since she had arrived in the hospital. The nurse said the doctor would be back in to fill me in on Carol's condition soon.

The nurse is here. Frank wonders how I am. She says I am doing well. The doctor comes in. Frank asks about my diagnosis. The doctor says I have had a TIA. I have not had a stroke. Frank asks about the results of the tests they have taken. The CT scan? The MRI? He explains they don't have that equipment. Frank asks where the closest ones are. He does not know. Maybe Prince George. Maybe Kamloops. Maybe Vancouver.

Obviously, the doctor feels it is not important for me to receive tests. Frank does not say he disagrees, but I sense he has reservations. The doctor tells Frank, "You can give her an aspirin. We can keep her a day or two; then you can drive her home."

The doctor leaves. I think Frank is not very comfortable with the doctor's ideas. I have no words to reassure Frank. I want to tell him I am comfortable. It is all right to wait until tomorrow to see if I am better. Frank says he is going to find a phone.

Frank:
He didn't know if it was a bleed or a clot and here they were giving her aspirin. I called John again for some sound medical advice. He said that I must sign her out against medical advice. The next call was to our son. I asked Tom if he could coordinate the evacuation from Vancouver to Bellingham since Canadian charters don't land in the USA. He said he'd started with our friends Dustin Hurlbut and Ron Peterson at the sheriff's office but hadn't been able to get hold of them. He was going to try a couple of other friends, but, if necessary, he'd make the trip himself.

Frank is gone a long time. He comes back to the room. He tells me the plan. The plan is very involved. He mentions people he has talked to.

Their names are faintly familiar, but I cannot place names to faces. I just know that many friends are helping Frank. He has talked to John, whoever that is. John says to get me home as soon as possible. Perhaps that is our good doctor friend and neighbor. John said to check me out of the hospital in Ft. Nelson. Frank is to hire a plane with a pressurized cabin. Frank is to get me home to St. Joseph Hospital in Bellingham as soon as possible.

Frank:
I started calling air charter services, looking for a twin engine pressurized cockpit plane so we would have IFR (instrument flight rules) and the pressurization would insure that Carol wouldn't have problems with cerebral edema. I quickly found a charter right there in Fort Nelson. I laid on the flight, gave the dispatcher my credit card number, and went looking for the doctor to get us signed out.

Leaving Fort Nelson

The nurse comes in. Frank says we want to check-out and that he has a flight scheduled. The doctor comes in. There are lots of words between them. I listen. I understand only snatches of the conversation. They are polite to each other, but they do not agree. The doctor seems insulted and embarrassed that Frank has chartered a flight to take me home. He attempts to salvage the situation by offering alternative transportation. They discuss other options to Frank's plan to hire a plane to get me home. I hear, "We could get her on a medical evacuation tomorrow or the next day. But with a TIA she's not a high priority. She would be on a waiting list." He asks the nurse about commercial flights. "How often do they come through Fort Nelson?"

Exasperated, Frank explains that I would feel more comfortable if I were in a familiar environment in my own hospital. Reluctantly, the doctor prepares discharge orders. Frank calls the air flight service to finalize arrangements for the flight.

He asks how soon they can be ready. Then bad words. "You can't? Why not? You'd agreed. If you cannot do it, can you give me the name of another flight service that could?" He listens. He looks around and pokes into his pockets as if to look for paper. I notice, also, that he has no pen. The nurse comes in. Nurses always have pens. I speak to her. Frank later tells me that what I say is, "He needs a wrench." She hears me. She has a pen, but she does not offer it to Frank. I repeat, "He needs a wrench." She hears me again, looking with a vacant stare. I point to Frank at the phone where he is still searching for a pen. She seems to understand. She gives Frank a pen. What was so hard about giving Frank a pen? Frank writes the phone number on his hand.

Frank:
I called the charter to arrange the pickup. He blandly told me that they had decided not to make the flight. Instead of blowing up, I asked him where I might find another flight since my wife was truly in a medical emergency situation. He gave me the number of a flight service in Fort St. John, 250 miles south. I called, quickly confirming that they had a Beech King Air 200. The charter fee would be $6500, and they would pick us up in 90 minutes with a litter on board. I then called Tom to see how he was doing with a ride from Vancouver to Bellingham. We agreed to meet at the Esso Avitat location, Vancouver International Airport, ETA 6:00 PM.

The nurse brings my clothes and an aspirin. Dressing uses all my energy. I fall back against the bed. Frank processes my discharge papers.

The nurse wheelchairs me to the back door next to the freight receiving dock. It is hot – very hot. A taxi is coming. I hope it is not very long. It is difficult to stay sitting up. The taxi does not come.

The nurse comes back to the door. "Hasn't the taxi come yet? I called them. I'll call again."

We wait. Again the nurse comes to the door. "Isn't he here yet?"

Finally the taxi shows up. The car is a rattletrap affair, but its back seat has to be more comfortable than the wheelchair. I am ready to collapse. We get into the back seat. It is very hot in the taxi. The driver seems to be in a hurry now to make up for lost time. Frank is still trying to find my seat belt.

The old crash-bang taxi groans and creaks as the cabbie drives all the quickest narrow winding backcountry roads to the airport. Frank holds me up to keep me from being thrown back and forth in the back of the taxi. In spite of the heat, I welcome his holding me up. I am too tired to sit up myself.

We get to the airport. The sun meets the tarmac, then rises in a visible shimmering heat wave. This is very hot. Hotter than any time during our Yukon River canoe trip. Hotter than it was inside the taxi. Far across the pavement is a plane that looks like the commuter planes I have taken from Bellingham to Seattle. Frank recognizes the plane as like the one we are chartering. I think it is too far away to walk there. It is too hot to walk that far. The plane will have to come closer to me or they will have to wheel me over there.

Frank is excited that our plane is here already. He throws some money at the cab driver and gathers me up. Puts me on my feet. Holds me up. He hurries me slowly across the baking blacktop with its too many steps. I do not think I can make it.

Frank takes us up to the steps of the side door of the plane. He talks to a man coming from the door and down the steps. It is not our plane. Frank is disappointed and disgusted with himself for making me walk all that distance for no reason. He holds me. I am too tired to walk back all that distance without resting. Frank feels that. He asks the man if I can rest on the steps. I rest there a few minutes to get my strength back. Then we walk the many steps back to the fueling station building.

It is a small station. We sit on the step of the porch in the sun. The brightness distorts my vision. It is very uncomfortable. Finally, Frank realizes it may be a while before our plane comes. It might be more comfortable inside the station. I collapse against the back of a couch, roll my head back against it and try not to look like I am completely wasted. I wonder if I look like I have had a stroke. What does a stroke victim look like?

Our plane lands. This time Frank waits for the pilot to come out. The pilot comes in and talks to the station man. He tells Frank they will have to fuel up so it will be a while. I am happy to rest some more before I have another long walk across the hot pavement. I sit and drink the ginger ale Frank got for me.

Our plane is nearer the station than the other plane was, but it is still a long walk. Frank is coming with me. He supports me to walk there. *How far will he come with me? Will he come with me to Vancouver?*

—∞—

The last time Frank actually flew on a commercial flight was in 1971 when he flew from Bellingham to Alaska to get to his job as a field geologist. I had spent my two-week vacation with him in the field. We mapped coal, flew fixed wings and helicopters from site to site and had a glorious time. He loved flying so much, he should have been a pilot. Catching our flight home in the Anchorage airport, however, it took Frank several drinks at the bar before we got into the plane to head home. I did not realize the significance.

The last time he was inside a large plane was 1978. We had driven to Indiana with our boys, Tom and Tim, when they were quite young to visit family. Frank planned to fly back home from Chicago to take care of our business while the boys and I drove back with my sister, Mary Jane, and her family.

In Chicago, he had walked up the jet way into the plane and found his seat. Then as they prepared to close the door, claustrophobia took over. The quarters were too confining. Panic overwhelmed him. He bolted for the opening. The stewardess tried to prevent him from leaving. "You can't leave," she said, "you must sit down."

He responded he had a phobia about flying, and he had to leave the plane. He stepped past the stewardess and proceeded back up the jet way to the gate. At the gate, there was some to-do about it being a problem to get his baggage out of the hold.

"We can't get your baggage out for you. You have to stay."

He told them to keep the luggage. He would just pick it up in Seattle when he got there.

"No," they said, "luggage must be accompanied by the passenger." They wanted to see his ID. In opening his wallet, the first card that came out was his permit to carry a firearm. The second card was his "blaster's" license. Suddenly, there was a circle of security officers surrounding him agreeing that he could leave the plane if he wished. And, "Yes sir, we will be getting your baggage out for you."

Frank was beside himself. He did not think to let us know his change of plans. There was no call from him at the end of the day. We left on our road trip wondering where he was. Each phone call attempt to Bellingham rang silent. On the third day, we learned he had taken the bus.

He was fine in a fixed wing over the mountains with his survival pack between his knees with a pilot he trusts. But the confines of a large plane and lack of control were different.

—◊—

This is not really a big commercial plane, but it is significantly larger than a two or four seater. Does this count as a large plane? Or is this a small plane? With each step up the ramp to the door, I wonder. *Will I have my husband with me?* I wonder if I will end up in the Vancouver airport by myself. How could I manage through the maze of a huge metropolitan international airport without help? I have been there before. Would past experience allow me to negotiate the airport alone? Without words? If I had energy? Possibly. If I had strength. But I have neither. No words. No energy. Probably not.

We are at the door. Frank is still by my side. I duck under the door. *Will Frank also pass the threshold? Or will he just give me a push into the plane and then retreat down the steps?* No. He comes inside with me. He helps me onto the litter. The copilot finds a blanket. They cover me and fasten me to the litter with a strap. The pilot and copilot ready the plane for takeoff. They close the door and move forward to the cockpit.

Frank sits in a seat next to the door and fastens his seatbelt. I watch him. I think he will go through with this flight. The props start up and start to move toward the runway. But we are still on the ground. Frank could still change his mind. He could go to the cockpit and ask them to take him back to the station. I watch. He seems resolved. Take off. We soar away. Frank has made the ultimate sacrifice.

Frank:
Those little turboprops have a terrific acceleration; we were in the air and heading south before I had a chance to be scared.

To Vancouver

I am comforted. I will not be alone in the Vancouver Airport.

My head has numb parts. I try hard to think clearly. Numbness prevents it – as an anesthesia that will not wear off. Each thought comes at an extraordinary mental expense. My brain strains at the effort. It needs to rest. It has been thinking too much.

I am not comfortable. My back aches. I cannot raise my knees against the strap. I squirm as I did on the helicopter. Frank comes over and loosens the belt. I try to prop up my knees. I try to stay warm under the one blanket. As we gain in elevation it gets colder. I do not see another blanket. I wish for my sleeping bag. The coldness seems to come from the bottom. I am too cold to sleep. I eye an empty seat. If I could sit in it, the seat would give more warmth than the litter. Maybe then the one blanket would be enough. I rise to get off the litter. Frank sees me. I nod to the seat. He helps me over to it. I cannot sleep sitting up, but I am more comfortable. I am warmer. Frank gives me the rest of my ginger ale.

Thoughts are but an obscured landscape. Invisible.

Frank:
We flew at 16000 feet. The sun was still shining and the spaces between the clouds gave us a good view of Prince George as we flew over. Then the soup got thick, and the pilots were using their Doppler radar to miss the worst of the clouds and turbulence the rest of the way to Vancouver.

Frank reads the landscape below for me as he would from a topographical map until thickening clouds obscure the landscape. Then, too, my thoughts drift through long periods of obscured thinking and short periods of clearing. With clarity, the landscape of thought is visible to me. But without words, my thoughts are blurred and to anyone else, invisible.

In fleeting periods of clarity, my mind wanders. Wonders about the future. Coming down from Whitehorse after the canoe trip, my mind had switched to work mode. I had organized my mind for the work I needed to do when I get home. I had a myriad of deadlines coming up. Tim would be coming back from the trade show in Salt Lake City. Then we would need to meet deadlines for pre-season orders. We had a sale coming up. I needed to get the mailing out. Tom handled most of the office work, but there were parts he did not like. I always did the sales tax. It would be due on the 25th. And the payroll? I needed to process it and get it to the bookkeeper.

Now my head wants order. It says to debrief. I need to debrief Tim from the trade show. Organize the pre-season deadlines. Get out the sale newsletter. Sales tax. Payroll. Can a numbed brain implement order without words? What if my mind does not clear quickly? If the TIA does not resolve to bring words tomorrow? What will be the implications? What impact will it have on our business? Our boys? My husband?

Vancouver Airport

Frank:
We popped out of the clouds over Georgia Strait on our final approach and made a beautiful, smooth landing, taxiing over to the Esso fuel depot. I looked through the window of the station and saw Tom's blond head – and knew we were on the way to the hospital.

We do not go to the main terminal. The plane rolls over to a smaller building. It has letters on it. The letters are "E-S-S-O". Tom with his white blond head is at the Esso door. Next to him is our good friend, Ramon Garcia.

Frank hustles me slowly to the Esso door. Tom and Ramon look seriously at me. I try not to look serious. I am okay. I think they see that. But, my brain is not. It does not make words. I think they do not see that.

Ramon brought his minivan. He brings it to the front door. He has removed the center seat. He has a pile of pillows and blankets on the floor. Frank and I get in the back seat. I pretend to be all right. I sit up with Frank. Ramon takes off before we can get our seat belts on. Ramon is all business. He drives fast. He moves in and out of traffic. He swerves in and out between cars. Back and forth between the lanes. Soon, my pretending fails. The pile of pillows and blankets beckons me to the floor. I dive for the pile. Pillow under my head. Blanket over me. *Ahhhh.* Sigh. Finally. Comfort. At last, fatigue collapses. I sleep.

Frank:
Ramon was booting his van down the freeway, passing in any lane that was open. Carol saw that he'd taken the middle seat out of the van and covered the floor with pillows and blankets.

With a great big sigh of relief, she curled up on the floor and was asleep. I was wondering how an American FBI agent could talk himself out of a ticket for driving like a wild man, but the RCMP was nowhere in sight.

At the border, the line was three hours long; Ramon had it all figured out ... he drove around on the right side, possibly using a little grass instead of blacktop, got into the Peace Arch Crossing Entry (PACE) lane and called the Port Director on his cell phone, explaining that he was a Federal agent, he had a critically ill friend on board, and would like to be cleared quickly through the PACE lane. We rolled past the booth, Ramon showed his FBI credentials, and we were on our way.

It only took 50 minutes from the airport to St. Joseph Hospital in Bellingham. We got in and were run through triage. Sixteen hours to get from the tent to the hospital; a trip I don't want to have to do again.

Part Two

St. Joseph Hospital

Admitting

I move to the edge of the door in the van. Frank will help me walk inside. No. He folds me into a wheelchair. He rolls me to the admitting desk. An official looking woman asks questions. A man comes to stand behind her. He asks questions of Frank. He looks at me. He questions me. I do not understand what he says. I could not have answered anyway, I am so weary.

I send a pleading glance to Frank that means he should answer the questions. Suddenly, the man rolls me into a back room. He puts me into a bed. He starts a series of tests.

> **Admit Time: 7:53 PM August 16, 1998**
> **Dr. Gregory Brown:**
> Patient came with her husband. When camping in B.C. last night at 2:00 a.m. became helpless. Speech unintelligible and right arm useless. It took until now to take an ambulance and helicopter to Fort Nelson B.C., then flew to Vancouver. Husband says speech has improved, able to walk now. Patient obeys commands. Right arm weaker than left. Some speech normal; some nonsensical.
>
> **Admitting Diagnosis:**
> Acute CVA with aphasia, etiology undetermined.

They hook me up with wires to a machine that reads me. It has moving lines. Many numbers. I hope it will show them how I need help. Most of the tests are done from the bed. Others require me to get up, stand or walk. Those are difficult. My body does not want to support me. Dr. Wu comes to represent our family doctor. He asks the same questions the ER doctor had asked.

Dr. Chao-Ying Wu:
The patient is a previously healthy vigorous female who had just completed a seven-day, 235-mile canoe trip down the Yukon and one of its tributaries with her husband. She awoke at 0200 with paresthesias to her face and she was able only to grunt, completely unable to form words. Her right arm was completely flaccid. She retained at least partial function of her right leg. Her husband notes that when he tried to help her into her clothing, she was able to move her right leg to assist him. It is unclear whether she had full function of the right leg at that time or not.

The paramedics in Canada noted a rapid irregular pulse but did not elaborate with further details. The patient has no history of atrial fibrillation nor hypertension. She has no known heart disease or prior cerebrovascular disease. There are no known autoimmune problems or vasculitides. She denied chest pain, symptomatic palpitations. She denies significant head trauma, but about six weeks prior, she did bump her head on a canoe strong enough to provide her with a black eye. There was no loss of consciousness.

Receptive language appeared fine. She had intermittent waxing and waning expressive aphasia. At times she was able to utter up to 4-5 complete grammatical and appropriate meaningful sentences in a row. At other times she spoke in fluent gibberish.

Soon the tests will tell me how and why I had this stroke. I had kept active but had not been on a regular exercise plan. Was I just out of shape? Should I have exercised more? And the birth control pill I had been taking to regulate my period during pre-menopause? I vaguely remember a warning in small print about stroke being a risk. I had been checked every year at the doctor's office to renew the prescription. Was that to give me warning I might be in danger of stroke?

They wheel me to a different room for x-rays. A man sets up the x-ray machine and asks if I can stand. *If you hurry,* I think. He puts me in front of the flat box. I slump against it and pull up on a bar to keep me from falling over. He asks me to move my body one way or the other or raise or lower my arms. He talks too fast. I do not understand the words. He has to show me what he wants me to do. Then I try to put it with the words.

The man looks at me and looks at my name and says, "You look familiar? Should I know you?"

He probably knows me from Base Camp, the specialty sporting goods store in the log building on Holly Street that my husband and I own.

He sees my inability to talk and says, "Never mind."

Never mind? Never mind! Like I do not count?

Then he says, "Your husband owns Base Camp, doesn't he?"

I own Base Camp, too, along with my husband.

Anger smolders and bursts into flames. Then flame falters when my suffocated word center finds no words. No words for a smart retort. Thought sees my fist meet his face. But both fists are needed on the bar to keep me upright. If my disgust could reach through my eyes that will be some satisfaction. But he does not see it in my eyes. My stroke makes my face unexpressive, frozen as wood.

Frank sits by me. He is almost asleep in the chair. I can see how tired he is. He has not slept since early morning. He has had nothing to eat since breakfast in Toad River. I am just as tired as Frank is, and I have been dozing at every opportunity since he woke me up in the campground. I want to tell him it is okay to go home. It is okay to go sleep. I know he needs to sleep. He can talk to the doctors in the morning. But I do not have those many words to tell him he can leave. He sits and dozes. I lie and doze between tests.

Dr. Wu comes in again. Yet, no answers. Laboratory tests: Normal CBC. Chest x-ray unremarkable. Head CT appeared normal. EKG showed normal sinus rhythm.

Assessment:
Neurologic deficit consistent with ischemia in the left middle cerebral artery distribution. Question whether this will be a prolonged TIA vs. RIND (reversible ischemic neurologic deficit) vs. CVA. Thus far she is on an improving trend and it's too

far off from the onset of symptoms so she is not felt to be a candidate for thrombolysis although we will continue to monitor closely through what we hope to be improvement.

A source of the neurologic event is unclear. Carotids and heart are normal to examinations, but it certainly does not rule out a source there. With a history of palpitations, I wonder if she may not have flipped in and out of a fib. (Her husband did note that she was tired the day before).

Plan:
She will be admitted to Telemetry and rhythm will be carefully monitored. She will take one enteric-coated aspirin per day. She will get a Doppler scan of the neck in the morning and, if negative, we will consider a TEE.

They have finished the tests they will do tonight. None of them show I have had a stroke. Or how. How can that be? Nevertheless, they will keep me in the hospital overnight to monitor me. Frank is free to leave. I am looking forward to something to eat, and I want to sleep.

Dr. Wu comes by before I am transferred to a room. He asks me questions. I try to respond. Some words come out correctly but more do not. They do not make sense. I wonder if I can write although I cannot speak. As a child I remember how I could write backwards by using my left hand. Since the stroke affected my right hand, might I be able to write with the left? I motion for paper and pencil.

Dr. Wu asks, "Do you want paper and pencil?"

I nod.

He goes, and after some time he comes back with paper and pencil. I try to write words with my right hand. No. My thoughts do not translate to the written word. The left hand? No. Not even if I try to write backwards. I shake my head. My brain is not generating words. To speak or to write.

The second day – I do not have my words back

Day dawns. It is raining. Cloud and fog meet the roof below. Rain splats on the roof. It falls on the air-conditioning and ventilation duct systems. That is my view. How long will it be before I return to the Yukon? Will I?

On the Yukon, I had been plagued with severe back pain. To be able to crawl out of the tent in the morning, I had to go through a series of back exercises Frank had given me. This morning in the hospital bed, I do the same exercises. My back is better. Perhaps sleeping on a bed has helped.

But this is not the good morning I had hoped for. My mind still does not think in words. The doctor at Fort Nelson must have been wrong. I have not had a TIA. This is more serious.

In spite of that, I cannot keep my mind off the Yukon.

—◊◊—

My sister, Betty Ann, and I approached a blind "S" drop behind Frank and Randy. They skirted the approaching turn and went to shore to see the drop first from shore. We started to follow their example. Then the drop came into view. The water was moving fast. The current made a gentle curve into a long strong "V". The "V" gathered in the distance resembling the tossing manes of many white horses. Beyond the waves in the distance the current cut right against a bluff.

"Betty Ann, I think we can make it!"

"Let's go for it!"

In an instant we turned the canoe into the current. We positioned ourselves in the center of the "V".

"Eeeeh-Haaaw!"

We rode it as the current rolled in from each side of the river. It curled into a raised crest of waving water. With low braces our canoe mounted the swelling current, and met the manes of the dancing white horses. We rode through. It was only a Class II, but it was exhilarating.

—◊◊—

In my hospital bed, I remember. My mind thinks and it remembers. How can it do that without words?

I look out the window. I cannot think of the word to say *cloud*. Neither can I say the words printed in the room. *St. Joseph Hospital*. A nurse comes in. I point to the clouds.

"hh-wWat — that?" pointing out the window making circular motions with my hands.

"The window?"

I say, "No," and make my circling motions again trying to point beyond the window.

Then she says, "Clouds?"

"Ahhh," I say, "Clouds." And I also try to remember about the *window* word.

I do not have my words back within the 24 hours the Fort Nelson doctor promised. However, I have not died overnight. I smile. I am alive. Two doctors come in together. I do not think of them as doctors. I recognize them as good friends and customers. I think that is nice. I beam. They must have been in on rounds and noticed I was here. They have come in to visit me as friends!

But, no. They are my doctors. Frank has arrived and he says, "Who's this?"

I know him. I say, "George."

George says, "No, Jeff."

As soon as he says his name, I cannot repeat it correctly.

"Never mind," he says.

They are amused I cannot remember their names. However, I sense they are personally concerned about me. They are to decide what to do with me next. I am to have an MRI. They may do something called a TEE. I may have had a paradoxical stroke. Either way, I can go home tomorrow. I think on that. I listen intently. I do not understand much of it. They talk too fast. The words are too hard. I think I get the gist of it but cannot repeat it. I cannot remember words without words in my head. Frank is here. He will remember. He can say the words to me again.

They give friendly smiles but no hopeful words about the future. Am I likely to have more strokes? Where might that lead? Will I learn words? What is my future if I cannot talk? Or read? Or write? The concerns are fleeting. My body is weary. I am not awake long enough to worry about a future of wordlessness.

A man wheelchairs me down the hallways. He pushes me very fast. He swings quickly around the corners. My head spins. I feel nauseous. I close my eyes around the corners to lessen car sickness. He rolls me to the MRI room. He leaves me in the hallway. He opens a large door. He goes inside. He comes back. He says, "They are not ready yet. It will be a few minutes."

I gaze at him.

He rolls my wheelchair to the center of the hallway some distance from the door to the MRI room. He locks the wheels. "I have to leave. Will you be okay here?"

I do not know if I will be okay here. Without words, I wonder how long a few minutes is. Without words, I wonder what if I have to go to the bathroom. Without words, I wonder how I will stay up in the chair if I get tired. Without words I cannot answer.

I gaze at him. He leaves.

I wait.

And wait.

And wait.

The door opens. People come and go. They leave me in the hallway.

I wait.

And wait.

And wait.

The door opens. They leave. They leave me in the hallway.

I am very tired. My head bobs. It wants a head support. I want to lie down. I want to sleep. My eyes close. To sleep. I weave. I jerk awake in starts. I am close to falling out of the chair. What shall I do? The hallway is empty. A corner is empty. It is out of the way. I can wheel the chair over there. I can get out and lay down on the floor. I can sleep on the floor. What will they think when they find me sleeping on the floor? I do not care. I move toward the corner.

The door opens. "We're ready for you now. I hope you haven't been waiting long."

My silent thoughts are not complimentary.

I sleep through the procedure.

MRI of the Brain:
There is an abnormal signal within the left temporal lobe cortex as well as within the insular cortex and the temporal or opercular cortex on the FLAIR and T2 weighted images consistent with a subacute cortical infarction in the posterior middle cerebral artery territory. No hyperintense T1 signal is present; therefore, there is no evidence of acute hemorrhage at this time. There is thickening of the cortex consistent with edema.

Impressions: Left posterior middle cerebral artery territory subacute infarction with edema.

MRI of the Neck:
There are no hemodynamically significant stenoses within either carotid artery. The carotid bifurcations are normal bilaterally.

Impressions: No hemodynamic stenoses either carotid bifurcation.

After I am back in the room, a doctor comes in. Dr. Stephen Malone is a cardiologist. I understand that has something to do with my heart. He explains they want to give me a TEE. Is that a word or three letters? Which letters? That is too many sounds for me to remember. Fortunately, his talk uses gestures to explain. I watch intently and listen carefully, but watching is the most productive. He also shows me a pamphlet. Between his gestures and the picture on the pamphlet, I have a sense of the procedure. They will put me nearly to sleep. They will push a tube down my throat. The tube will go down my throat until it reaches beneath my heart. There they will be able to "see" my heart.

"No lunch," he says, "you need an empty stomach."

I have been looking forward to lunch.

I do not know why it is important to see my heart. What does it have to do with the stroke in my brain? I hope they know what they are doing. I look at the pictures in the pamphlet many times. On the cover, words are printed, *Transesophageal Echocardiogram (TEE).* The cross-section picture shows a person lying down with a tube in their throat until it lies under the heart. I look at the words. The letter patterns of *esopha* I recognize as letters representing the throat. The letter patterns of *cardio* I recognize as representing the heart. None of it translates to the spoken word.

There is not much else I can do between naps. I cannot read a magazine. I cannot read signs. I cannot even eavesdrop on conversations in the hallway. But I can watch. It is still raining. The unattractive roof top landscape below, however, is improved by the many beautiful bouquets on my windowsill.

The word of my stroke must have traveled quickly. I gaze on the flowers in great appreciation. I did not know so many people knew me or cared for me. There are cards, too. I cannot read them. Sometimes I recognize the pattern of the letters on the signature to match it with a family member. More often, Frank has to explain to me who the card is from.

And I walk. I gather up my little telemetry box with its wires into a little pocket in my hospital smock. The box is very heavy. It is hard to keep my smock closed over my breasts and over my tail end. But walking is better than staying in bed between naps. I am unsteady, but I try to hide that. I learn the pattern of the hallways on my floor. I look at all the signs and wonder what they say.

The kids come by. Tim is back from the trade show in Salt Lake City. Tom is back to business at the store now after coordinating my evacuation yesterday. It feels good to have hugs from them and to be alive. I don't have enough words to talk with them, but the family love among us speaks.

Underneath, there are worrisome thoughts in my mind that do not show and I cannot say. Both boys are going to take the brunt of running the business. We do not know how long it will take me to recover from this stroke. We do not know if I will recover. If I do not learn to talk, and read, and write, I will be of little use in the business. Also, Frank will be preoccupied with me and have less time in the store. This is a bad time for the boys. They both need to move on to establish lives of their own. But they will feel obligated to take care of their parents' business.

My mind is in a state of mild anxiety. There are jobs in the store I do with no one else realizing. How am I going to be able to tell the boys to do them and give them instructions? I need to get to the store. Perhaps then I can pull out filing drawers and pull up folders to show them what to do. I think I can do that. I think I will recognize the folders that represent the work that needs to be done. Our bookkeeper can help them. What is her name?

Frank is feeling the pressures of unknowns as well. He does not say so, but after almost 30 years of marriage he does not have to. He comes in during the day when he can leave the store and at night. Tonight the phone rings. He answers. Frank does not say who calls. *Is it for me?* I would love to hear the voice of one of my friends. I would love them to visit me in the hospital. His voice shows me that he is very worried about me. Emotional overtones permeate the room.

"She is doing all right."

"No, she doesn't talk very much."

"No, she shouldn't see visitors. She is too tired."

"Don't come see her."

As he hangs up, I ask "Who — that?"

"It was Irene."

The sound he uttered does not seem to fit to anyone I know. "Who?"

"Irene, you know, your good friend Irene Rinn."

"Ahhh." With that, I am able to put an image of a person with the name.

I see now that Frank is protective of me. He is right. I am still very tired. At the same time, I would enjoy seeing Irene.

Irene:
The beginning, of course, is the moment when I listened to my voicemail and heard Robin's voice saying, "Carol has had a stroke." She said she had been in your store and overheard a staff person telling someone that you were not back home yet but were to be transported to Vancouver and then home to Bellingham. It was late at night when I got the message, and my mind filled with fear crowded by memories, vivid images of the places you have held in my life over the years: brewing tea on

our cross-country ski outings, camping with my kids, practicing canoeing for Ski to Sea, camping and canoeing in Canada, reading **Kidnapped** out loud when camping, swimming at Fairy Slipper Island, the Yellow Aster Meadows swim with ice chunks in the water, the Pacific Crest Trail hike – you sighting on the mountain peaks to find our way, and so much, much more over days and years.

The next day I call and hear you are back in town, in the hospital – but Frank says not to go to see you yet – you are so fatigued. I get some information, but so little is clear – there is much they do not know. So I wait, having told Frank I will check in again tomorrow.

The third day – discovery day

It is not a good night. There is a loud party in the hallway. Maybe it is not a party. But there is a lot of loud talking, coming and going by my open door all night. And just as I am about to doze off, a nurse checks on me – to take my blood pressure – my temperature – to arrange the telemetry wires which were attached to patches all over my body. Unsettled thoughts prevent sleep.

It is not a good morning either. As the day dawns, it is still raining and foggy. I can see that I will not be able to see past the ugly array of air conditioner boxes and duct systems on the roof below me.

In frustration, with squinted eyes, I let out a large yawn. "Eee — aaahhhhhhh!!!!"

With that I open my eyes, and see three attendants surrounding my bed. In the blink of the eye they are here! They must think I am in dire need.

Each morning, they check to see that I have not had another stroke. So, do my eyes follow their finger? Squeeze my hands with their fingers. "Tighter." I do not want to hurt their hands. "Tighter." Then my legs. "Push." "Pull." They want me to press or pull my foot against their hands. But I do not understand. They talk too fast. They don't give me time to think about each direction. "Push?" "Pull?" I have to think about the words to make sense of them. They do not have time. They show me which way to move my feet.

The morning nurse comes in to see if I have any more words than yesterday. "Do you know where you are?"

Of course I do. "Yes." My boys were born here. I had taken them to the emergency room with chisel and axe cut accidents before they were old enough to go to school. I had surgery here to repair a broken finger. I visited Tim here the week he spent in the burn unit. I was here with Frank's broken heels. I had an appendectomy here two years ago after the 1996 Yukon canoe trip. "Yes."

"Where are you?"

I can only point around the room.

Again, "What is the name of this place?"

She is persistent considering I have too few words. Exasperated, I point to the sign on the wall. The sign shows the *St. Joseph Hospital* words I cannot say.

"What is your name?"

"Carol."

"Do you have children?"

"Yes."

"How many?"

I show two fingers.

"What are their names?"

I shrug.

Frank comes in. The nurse says, "Who is this?"

I smile. Of course, I know him. This is my husband. She knows that. She just wants me to say his name. I cannot think of his name. I pause. I stutter. I buy time. Still I cannot remember the sounds that make his name. Finally, something comes. It blurts out, "Pard." It sounds right. How did I come up with it?

Frank smiles. "That is our nickname for each other," he explains to the nurse. There is another nickname I use for Frank, but I do not remember it.

Dr. Glenn [fictitious name] orders one more test before I am to be discharged. It will involve an ultrasound. Since the TEE required a wheelchair ride to another section of the hospital, I expect to leave the room again. But a man comes into my room with a machine on a rolling cart and does it while I am in the bed. He probes my right leg and then my left. After he probes behind my left knee, he quickly loads up all the ultrasound equipment and leaves the room saying, "Good luck."

Ultrasound report:
Vas Venous Duplex Bil+

Indications for Procedure: Patient with a patent foramen ovale and CVA, rule out deep venous thrombosis.

Impression: Superficial phlebitis with thrombus extending in the proximal lesser saphenous system to the popliteal vein where there was demonstrated small emboli with distal leg compression.

As soon as the vascular technician gets his equipment out the door, my nurse, Susan, is wheeling in new equipment. I want to get out of the bed and stretch and walk around. Susan, says, "I don't think the doctor will want you to be active right now."

I point to the bathroom.

She thinks and reluctantly says, "Okay, you can go to the bathroom."

Back at the bed, Susan has an IV stand and needles ready for me. She starts to insert the IV. I think she is making a mistake. "— Go — home. — Doctor — say — go — home."

She says, "I think the doctor will want you to stay a few more days."

"hh-Wat? That?" (Nodding to the IV apparatus.)

"Yes," she says, "a few days."

I am not happy.

As she is taping the IV to my arm, I have visions of having a sloppy arrangement of tapes and tubes fastened to my arm. I am fussy. If I have that IV hooking on to me for a few days, I want it to look good and be comfortable. I manage to command, "Do good."

She replies she will do a neat job, and she does.

Frank and Dr. Glenn show up at the same time. Dr. Glenn shows us the MRI images with the cloudy area where my stroke occurred. He says I have had a CVA, not a TIA. Then he tells us the TEE showed I have a significant hole in my heart called a patent foramen ovale (PFO).

> **Transesophageal Echocardiogram:**
> **Indication:** A 53-year-old lady admitted with expressive aphasia. Transesophageal echocardiography was performed to assess for possible cardiogenic embolic source.
> **Findings:** The microbubble contrast solution study show evidence for a patent foramen ovale.

The PFO is between the right and left sides of the heart. He gestures with his hands and draws a picture to show the position of the heart and the hole between the right and left atrium. Then he explains that I am still throwing clots. The clots are behind my knee. Those clots go up to the right side of the heart. Ordinarily, blood from the lower extremities returns to the right side of the heart and then through the lungs to be oxygenated before it goes to the left side of the heart. From there, the heart pumps the blood into the arterial network. Ordinarily, clots from the lower extremities collect in the lung. But if the clots from the lower extremities meet resistance at the lung, sometimes the returning blood is forced back through the patent foramen ovale short-cutting the venous blood to the left atrium. If there are clots in the blood, a clot will plug an artery, stopping the supply of oxygen to that area. Cells in that area die from lack of oxygen.

That is a lot to think about. I get the idea of what he was saying, but there is no way I can repeat it or ask questions about it. I ask and motion, "Write?" I need to see what he has said. Then Frank can tell me again. If I learn to read, I could read the words myself.

Dr. Glenn's notes:
1. Likely cause of stroke:
   a) prolonged sitting → deep vein thrombosis (DVT) (L) leg
   b) clot forms → breaks off → goes to (R) side of heart
   c) goes from (R) → (L) side of heart B/O "hole" (patent foramen ovale)
   d) clot goes to brain → "stroke"

2. Less likely cause:
   a) hx [history] of migraine hd's [headaches]
   b) plus estrogen / BCP's [birth control pills]
   c) spasm + "stickiness" → clot →
   d) brain → stroke
3. Both quite rare / unusual!
4. Doing better! Probably anti-coagulate 2 to 3 days in hospital, + then dlc'd on Coumadin = blood thinner.

The IV drips heparin to dissolve the clots so I will not have another stroke. In the meantime, I am not supposed to move around much. I wonder why the lower extremity venous ultrasound was the last thing they did. It was clearly the easiest and most definitive test done. It reveals the most life threatening condition I have. I have been throwing clots ever since my stroke. That has been almost two and a half days. It is a wonder I have not had another stroke.

From Dr. Braun we learn more. The PFO (patent foramen ovale) can be closed by open heart surgery and possibly by other methods. He says I do not have to do that right away. I should wait a year. In the meantime, I will be on Coumadin to keep my blood thinned. Coumadin is warfarin. Warfarin is rat poison. Frank speaks in my place that open heart surgery is not an option for me since I am a Jehovah's Witness and will not take blood.

What? Speak for yourself. I know that Witnesses commonly have open heart surgery without blood transfusions. If open heart surgery will close the PFO and eliminate the necessity of eating rat poison forever, I will consider it.

And now I wonder some more. How can I have reached the age of 53 with a significant PFO and not had a stroke before? Dr. Glenn emphasizes the clot formation was due to prolonged sitting in the canoe. But his theory does not follow. I had taken longer and more arduous canoe trips as an Outward Bound instructor for three seasons in my twenties. If prolonged sitting in a canoe for hours were responsible for my stroke, I would have had a stroke long ago.

As for my being able to talk again? Dr. Braun says about 50% of my total recovery will occur in the first six months. About 85% of my total recovery will occur by the end of the first year. He says I can take speech therapy. Then adds that he questions the value of it. Most people do not get much out of it.

Dr. Braun said six months. Without realizing it, my damaged word center translates six months to six weeks.

This sets my head spinning. In the first six weeks? He said six weeks! That is not very much time to learn half of what I need to learn! How can anyone relearn most of an adult's collection of words in six weeks? Heck, how long did it take me as a kid? Counting since birth, it probably took 12 years to be able to read the *Reader's Digest* comfortably! And I have to be half-way there in six weeks? Then even after a year, I will have basically gained only 85% of all I will ever relearn. What about the remaining 15%? The implication is that after a year, my brain function will have little improvement.

I am alone in the room with the IV stand and a machine that beeps when the bag runs out. I gaze at the windowsill with its ever growing display of flowers and cards. I close my eyes to rest. When I open them, Irene is coming over to my side. I do not know how to say her name, but I am so glad to see her. All I can do is put my arms out for a hug. So much to tell about and so very few words to say it. She said Tim said it would be all right to visit me. He told her that if she spoke slowly I might understand what she said. The visit is brief. She promises to come back. It leaves me in better spirits.

Irene:
I walk in and you reach for a hug, pulling the same doleful face that at times you have pulled for much lesser things. Now it says so much and I find you can say so little. I say how glad I am that you are back here and I find immediately that you do not understand. I try to speak slowly. You still do not understand although I think that you know I am expressing concern. I try to ask you some slow questions and you cannot answer. I sit and say a few things slowly, and I can see in your eyes that sometimes you understand my words, but often you are bewildered by them. Others come to visit and I slip out saying slowly that I will come back.

I am in a predicament. Should I feel sorry for myself? A tear rolls down my cheek. I think. That's dumb. Crying will not help. I could pray. I should pray. To whom shall I direct the prayer? God? The word *God* finds no place in my mouth. My mouth forms various shapes in search of the sounds that speak the name of my God. Finally, quietly, the sounds say, "Jehovah." Yes, that is my God. "Jehovah." That is prayer enough.

I really do not have very many words. What am I going to do with the rest of my life if I do not regain my vocabulary? Unless this stroke gets worse, I will not be in a nursing home. I will be at home. Can I manage without words? I would be happy doing woodworking down in the basement. Maybe this is a blessing!

Then I visualize the things I would do. The first thing would be to adjust the blades on the planer, and adjust the blades and the in-feed table on the jointer-planer. Then I think. That is always a tedious process and I have always had to follow directions in the manual to do it. Without being able to read, trying to figure it out myself will be even more difficult.

And what about when I want to buy lumber? I am accustomed to going back into the stacks in the lumber yard. I look over the stack and pick out the boards I want. I can do that without words. But what if they ask me a question? What shall I say? And what if I want plywood? I do not know the types of plywood. I always have to ask or look it up in a book beforehand. How will I ask for help? Will I know the words to make the question? More importantly, how will I understand what the clerk is telling me?

And finishing materials? I would have to know about finishing material. Before, I could always go to a book or *Fine Woodworking* magazine to find my answers. Then, I would go to the store and read the properties of the finish on the back of the can and talk to the clerk. Now I cannot.

The world revolves on words

What is this odd feeling that haunts me? It is almost as though I am watching a movie with no sound or with subtitles I cannot read. It is almost as if I am deaf though I hear. My head does not hurt. But, it does not feel right. It feels hollow. It is as if my ears are filled with cotton. Everything that filters through them echoes indistinctly in the empty space beyond. In the void, word sounds float. It is true a few words find a landing place, and I can receive the word sounds. However, it is very few.

For most, there is no landing place and without it, I cannot catch them. The search for words is endless.

Huge quantities of energy are spent searching. This is hauntingly familiar. Why?

Then it comes to me.

—‿—

On the porch of our apartment, my father was building a bed for me from an Army surplus cot frame and a collection of salvaged lumber. He was using hand tools. I watched intently.

Seeing my interest, he said, "Carol, do you want to help Daddy?"

I nodded.

"Carol, this is a hammer. Give Daddy the hammer."

I gave Daddy the hammer.

"Carol, this is a screwdriver. Give Daddy the screwdriver."

I gave Daddy the screwdriver.

"This is a brace and bit." I nodded.

"This is a drill." And I nodded.

"This is a saw." And I nodded.

My young brain raced to remember the new words. It listened and concentrated to grasp the new words. To encompass them. My brain strained with its every force.

Then, Daddy said, "Carol, give Daddy the drill."

I thought very hard. *Drill.* I looked for the tool he told me was a drill. I handed it to him.

"Carol, Daddy needs the saw."

"Saw?" I thought hard to remember what the saw was. I saw it. I handed it to Daddy.

I was three years old.

—‿—

Today, I am 50 years older. At the same time, I am three. My brain strains as it did when it was three years old. My mind's word skill level is that of a three year old. The other parts of my brain store the experiences of half a century with no words.

Naively, I believe it will be easy enough to learn my missing words again. I assume that as I learn the new words, I will also recognize them when they are spoken to me. I will do it as I did when I was three years old. I will listen to the words people say to me. I will try to repeat them. I will listen to the conversation between people. I will try to pick out words I need and repeat them. I need words; the world revolves on words. Some I have picked up already: *yes, no, please, thank you, bathroom, good.* A good start.

The day is old now and I am tired. However, dinner offers an opportunity to learn new words. Tonight, the food tray comes with real food I can chew on and an appetizing dessert. Looking at the menu, I can associate some words with the items on the tray though I cannot say them. One is coffee. I hate coffee. I take it off the tray and give it back to the nurse. In a hospital setting, the smell often turns my stomach. Tea is what I like. But I cannot say it. I know that even if I can ask for tea, it will not be good. The hospital kitchen serves it in plastic coffee cups. It tastes like coffee. But that is okay. I can live without tea. What captures my attention is the dessert. I search up and down the menu to identify it on the page. It is the one with the letters, "C-h-o-c-o-l-a-t-e P-i-e." *Mmmm.*

Irene appears. It will be good to have her here for company while I eat. *I should share.* But no, I am not going to share my dessert. I am going to enjoy that after I eat the main course. She can help me with the words, though. I point out the chocolate pie on the menu saying, "Y — y — yum!"

She asks if I can say it.

I say, "No."

So, Irene sounds out for me, "choc-o-late pie."

"Ahhh, — ch-oc-o-late." The *chocolate* part of the phrase proves a lasting impression. Mentally in my head and physically in my mouth I try to remember the sound that comes when I see "ch." Then I use the chocolate word in my mind to get my mouth set up to say it. The pie part? That is too much to remember at one time. The pie part, I promptly forget.

Irene:
For the first of many times to come, I am struck by the enormity of this – that you know and yet the words cannot come. This is my first indication of how confounding this is. We attempt to talk, and it takes great effort for you – long silences, clearly struggling to recall and say simple words, most not coming at all.

The evening shift nurse taking care of me is an Indian. An India Indian complete with an accent. She is all business and difficult to understand. She has a long name on the staff ID card that does not resemble any English letter patterns I ever imagined. Looking at the tag, I try to say her name. She says, "Call me Rai." After dinner there is a lull. I try to take advantage of it by relaxing. But no, Rai thinks it is time for me to clean up.

"No," I say, "bed." Meaning, I will clean up at bedtime.

Rai does not agree. "Don't you want to look nice for your husband when he comes? Don't you want to be pretty for him?"

Pretty? For my husband? My husband loves me more sincerely than appearances. He prefers me without make-up or perfume. Besides, I am clean; I took a shower this morning. Of course, my silent gaze does not tell her that.

Rai is insistent. I wonder what I will do to look pretty for my husband. Getting cleaned up to look pretty is more complicated with the addition of the heparin IV bag. I rise from the bed away from the sink. That side is where the IV apparatus is. My hand is tethered to the IV bag which is tethered to a big box on the stand that is tethered to an electric cord to the wall. Threading through the tubes and cords is like uncoiling a nest of snarled monofilament fishing line. Stand up. Unplug the cord from the wall. Arrange the lines. Grab the stand and roll it with me to the other side of the bed to the sink and mirror. Into the mirror I gaze. Rai hands me a hot washcloth as a hint I could start by washing my face. I go through the motions. I do not think it makes me look pretty. Neither do I think I am any cleaner. However, it does feel good.

It reminds me of waking up from a back-country campout. Frank always heats up a pot of water. He pours the scalding water over a bandana or washcloth so we can wipe our faces with it. *Ahhh. That is the life. Not even the rich people have it any better.* So, Rai's hot washcloth does feel good. For a moment I bathe in the luxury of it. Then brush my teeth and comb my hair. I am done. Rai looks for my make-up and perfume. Not seeing even a tube of lipstick in my toilet kit, she lets me retreat to the bed.

Frank:

All this time, Carol was still looking a bit stunned; she was so tired, she would sometimes drop off to sleep while we were talking. Much of the evening shift there was an Indian nurse (from India) who spoke such broken English that it was hard to understand what she was trying to say. Carol really had a time with her speech, but she was so cheerful and upbeat that the net result was positive. Near the end of the week, she told me that my wife was a beautiful, strong woman and that she would undoubtedly get well. Coming at a time like that, I really appreciated the thought.

Another day blends into the rest – hospital rhythm and learning more what I do not know

On Wednesday, I need less sleep and begin to notice hospital life has an almost predictable rhythm. An orchestrated rhythm accented with dissonance.

Needing sleep desperately, I vow to ignore all those nighttime interruptions. Even in sleep, though, I sense when someone comes in. The door opens. A light turns on. Someone checks the IV apparatus. Someone comes in. Turns on the light. Takes my blood pressure. Takes my temperature. Someone comes in, turns on the light and presents a blood draw basket. No problem. I never mind blood draws. Drowsily, I let her have my arm and drop off back to sleep. This gal must have been new at the job. Drowsily, I ignore the pain from her poking the needle around repeatedly to find a vein.

In the morning while doing my back exercises, I wonder why I have a new stiff joint. Even laying in bed my inner elbow throbs. Then I look. The bruise is huge!

"Oh dear," my favorite morning nurse, Susan, says. "The heparin and the Coumadin must have caused a bleed from the blood draw."

It was not the blood thinner. The blood draw lady did not know what she was doing! "No! — She — no good!"

Before the stroke, I had been on birth control pills to regulate my period. Sunday morning of the stroke would have been the last pill in the compact. That means that at any time, my period will start. This also adds another sense of anxiety and urgency. I need words. *Period* and *Tampax* are not in my vocabulary.

Fortunately, my nurse, Susan, thinks ahead. She asks if I will be menstruating and if I will need supplies. "Yes," I reply. No problem now. She will take care of me. She must have worked with wordless patients before.

Unfortunately, Susan comes back with one Kotex type pad. It is one of those old fashioned ones to be held up with a sanitary pad belt. But no belt. Somehow I express my concern about needing a belt. Susan goes away to look for a belt. When she comes back her hands are empty. The hospital does not supply belts with the sanitary napkins. Neither do they have the stick-on type pads or tampons. My anxiety is compounded.

I know there is a drug store across the street from the hospital. I could just walk over there and pick up a box of Tampax. If I have the energy to walk that far. And if I were not tethered to this confounded IV apparatus. Frank becomes my only hope. When he comes in to see me, I show him the pad and stammer around enough so that he comes to understand I need Tampax. I think he will go buy some Tampax and bring them right back to me. But, somehow, he does not understand my urgency. Fortunately, my period has not started yet when he returns most of the day later, having come back from home with two Tampax.

Two? I could go through two in an hour or two if I have a gusher. And I need secure pads, too, just in case. I cannot be upset. Frank is trying. He just does not understand my problem, and I cannot make myself be understood. Frank says he will bring more, but when?

By the next morning, my period has started and I am desperate for more Tampax. I have kept a Tampax wrapper with the word *Tampax* on it to help me say it. If I look at the word, sometimes I can say the word. Other times, not. It is worth a try. With the wrapper in hand, I call Frank on the phone to say, "Tampax. Tampax. Tampax." He will understand I need more and will bring them when he comes to town.

Lifting the phone, I look at the buttons. The phone has a strange feeling about it. It should be familiar. It is not. Using the phone had been instrumental in running my business. How do I use this now? It should be second nature. Punch buttons. Do I remember the phone number? Frank will be home at this time. I will call home. I look at the numbers on the buttons. I let my hand pass over the buttons in an ingrained pattern.

1-2-3-4-5-6-7.

Frank does not answer. It is not even a person on the other end. It is the hospital automatic messaging system. It speaks words of instruction to me. The words it speaks do not make sense. I do not know what the words say. Exasperated, I hang up. This cannot be this difficult. When I was in the hospital before, how did I make the phone work? When I have been in a motel, how have I made the phone make calls out?

Maybe if I push "9" first I can reach Frank.

9-1-2-3-4-5-6-7.

The message machine makes more words I do not understand. I try the number again dialing "0" first and then, "1". Always the confounded message lady jabbers at me words that make no sense to me.

The phone idea will not work. I cannot reach Frank this way.

Words — words — I need words

Being in the hospital puts learning words on hold. The doctors and nurses work primarily to stabilize my blood to an acceptable anticoagulation threshold. When that is reached, I can go home. In the meantime, I have enough time between naps to ponder. Why is my brain able to function in some ways yet not in others? More importantly, I ponder about what still works in my brain. Why does it function in some ways? Why will a word spontaneously pop out occasionally? And others not at all? I had always been taught that the brain had a finite number of cells and if any of those cells are lost, they do not grow back. How am I going to learn to talk again if those cells are dead? They speak of my words coming back. Where are they coming from? Dead brain cells are nothing. How can I access nothing – a void?

Time is ticking by. Though wordless, my mind races. The learning deadline is being used up to no avail. No one is helping me learn words. Seemingly, no one cares. It is up to me. How can I help myself without the brain matter to do it? Each hour that passes without learning is an hour lost against the six week limit I misinterpreted for achieving the 50% recovery benchmark. Is there anything I can do on my own without a teacher? What is left in my brain? What are my resources?

I can listen. I listen to all the words spoken to me and around me. Maybe some of the words will stick. I try to use them. I have listened to Frank tell the stroke evacuation story many times. I try to tell the story to anyone who will listen. Most nod up and down as if they understand. Then move on to a new subject. Others look at me inquisitively saying at the end, "I don't know what you are saying." Nevertheless, I keep jabbering. I do not know how to talk except to keep trying. Am I jabbering as Grandfather Schultz did after his stroke? He never learned to speak again.

Frank gives me updates on what is going on at the store. He talks about the people who have come by the store who are interested in me. I grasp at the words as he talks to me. I try to grab them so I can use them myself later. It is hard. With one story I come away with one word. Bear.

Frank says that Randy is back from the campground in northern British Columbia. Randy brought the camping equipment from the campground with the van. Frank said there were no Flapjacks (a home-made oatmeal cookie from the Minnesota Outward Bound School) or any Johnson's Crossing's famous cinnamon buns left. Randy ate them all. Frank says Randy could not get into the campground right away. When he got there after sending us off in the ambulance, Randy found the campground closed. Between the time we left the campsite to find help and when Randy got back, a grizzly bear had raided the campground. The bear had torn up several campsites and been a threat to the campers while eating up as much food as it could. The campground had been closed until they could remove the bear. To think I had wanted to stay at the campsite while Frank and Randy went for help! There could be worse things than having a stroke; I could have been eaten by a grizzly bear. Frank tells the story only once. That is not often enough for me to be able to repeat the words.

Listening is entertaining, but it is not teaching me how to say words. Listening is not enough. Desperately, I gather my collections of tubes and cords in search of learning. With rolling IV stand in hand, I prowl the hallways. Prowling for what I do not know.

Slowly, I walk the loop. There are not many patients walking around on this floor. Most of the patients are in worse shape than I am. The signs on the walls still do not say words to me. I study the pattern of the hallways in my section and venture out to other parts of the hospital on this floor. I have to remember myself how to get back to my room through a maze of intersecting passages. I cannot ask directions if I get lost. I cannot say who I am, or even that I am lost.

Ahhh, a lobby. That is where families wait. Maybe there will be a puzzle for children to use. Maybe there will be children's books. Maybe something there will speak to a numbed brain. No, nothing there speaks to a numbed brain. There are magazines that speak to a normal brain, but not to mine. Peeking through a window into a courtyard, I am at least entertained. Here is a place I can see real trees and plants. When I am bored, I can come back to this place and watch. Slowly retracing my adventures, I take myself back to my room and collapse on the bed.

Aaargh! Here comes the blood draw basket. In spite of having ice on my arm all day, the bruise is still a swollen mess. I do not know if this lady is the same one who did me before, but I am suspicious. I distrust anyone with a blood draw basket. I jabber, "You? — You — good? — Good, good? — Only — one! Only — one!" She thinks I am out of my mind. I am. She takes one look at the bruise from the last blood draw and gets the message. She wonders, too, if she can find a vein and calls on Susan. Susan approaches the blood draw site with confidence. I do not know how she will find the vein hidden within the swollen tissue.

Quietly, I say, "#?*%!" Susan smiles because she does not expect me to curse. I am surprised, too. I seldom do. I do not even know what word I used, but I know it was a curse word. Somewhere in the depths of wordlessness the most profane come forth so easily.

After Susan has found the vein easily, I ask, "More?"

"Yes, the doctor will want to have more blood draws."

"You? — You?"

"No, I will probably not be here the next time. The next time will probably be tonight."

"You. — You tell. — Find good one. — One time!"

With that I hope Susan will put out the word that I want only a good blood person to do my blood draw.

I point to the television. I have exhausted the possibility of finding available resources for learning words and find less need to sleep. I am bored. I want to know how to turn it on. The nurse shows me how the buttons on the remote work.

I want to find the TV show the boys used to call *Sesame Street*. We do not have a television at home so I do not know if it even shows anymore or at what time. But I do remember when Tom and Tim were preschoolers visiting Grandmother's house, they were able to watch *Sesame Street*. Sometimes the show taught letters and words to the preschoolers. That is what I need.

I do not find *Sesame Street*, but better than that, a speech therapist walks into the room. This is a surprise to me and I am excited that this is going to be my first lesson to learn words! I turn off the television, eager to learn from the speech therapist. The lady introduces herself. Her name erases itself from my brain almost as soon as she says it. I look for her name tag hoping to find her name written there, but it is turned over. That is okay. Since she is going to be my speech therapist, I will be seeing her again and will be able to learn her name. The lady talks to me about being aphasic and gives me pamphlets.

Aphasia. So that is what my wordlessness is called. Aphasia: *without speech.* She says the pamphlets would be helpful to me. Does she know I cannot read? She says my family should read them, too. *Maybe they will read it to me.* Then she pulls out some flash cards and takes notes. This is a test so I try very hard. The cards have pictures on them with words under them. I am supposed to say what the pictures are. They are easy pictures. Car. Tree. Chair. Ball. Dog. The pictures are familiar. I know what they are. The words are not easy. I do not know words to go with the pictures. The lady corrects my efforts and tells me the words. She allows me to repeat them one time as if that is enough. I want to learn them. I expect the role of a speech therapist to teach me the words; to drill with me to help me learn. But no drill, just testing. I am disappointed. My heart joins the vacancy of my brain. Empty brain; now empty heart.

I go back to the television. That is also disappointing. The television says words too fast. I do not understand the words. I flip the channels trying to find some more slowly spoken words or pictures that linger instead of flashing by too rapidly. It is exhausting to concentrate on the television. I rest.

In the evening, I try to watch the television again. It has words and it has pictures. Maybe if I look at it often enough, I will learn some of the words. This is a weather channel. The weather man talks to me from the screen. A moving line of words crosses the bottom of the screen. Are the words in the moving line the same words the man is saying? This is not the same as watching television for entertainment when we are in a motel room during a trade show. This is work.

A weather map appears. The man talks and waves his hands over the map as weather symbols move across the continent. Major cities are marked with their names. The man says the names of the cities. He talks about the kind of weather as it moves across the United States. But he talks too fast. The moving map moves too fast. I recognize the cities. That city is Bellingham where we live. That is Seattle. That one is near my friend in Iowa. That one is near my sister and an aunt in Illinois. That one is near my father in Indiana. That one is near my other sister in Massachusetts. Here and there, I have friends and experiences at one place or another. I try to remember the important city names. The man says a city name, but while I am trying to remember how to say it, he has moved on to the next three cities and I have forgotten the first. I visualize the family members scattered across the nation. But they are only images in my mind. The names of my sisters, Mary Jane Bohall and Betty Ann Giles, the name of my Aunt Helen or the name of my father, Ed Cline, do not come to mind.

The next show is a story. I remember hearing there was a television serial based out of Vancouver, British Columbia. This must be it. The scenes look like Vancouver. There is a lot of dialog. I feel compelled to watch with the hope I will learn words from it. More talk. I catch enough from the talk that the story has something to do with treasure or a mine. There is a bad guy and some good guys. There is a gun and a fight. There is deception. From the music, I feel when there is a sense of secrecy and suspense. But I never truly understand the story. There is a long boat trip up a large river to a small town and a secret cave. I don't catch the place names, but I look at the scenes carefully. They are familiar places. I grasp at any familiarity to see if a word will come or to reinforce the notion of where it is produced. The scenes scan quickly, the dialogue faster. My brain scans on slow. The trees? What are they? Are they northwestern trees? I do not see enough at first. I wait until the forest scene comes again. That looks like a stand of Doug Fir. Later, another forest scene – a Western Red Cedar? Will there be a close-up that allows me to actually see the needles? No, all I need is to see the overall pattern of the bough, or the overall shape of the tree or a scene with one of the actors passing the bark of one of the trees to show me what kind it is. My mind recognizes pictures.

Learning the "bear" word

This is one of those educational shows. It is taken out-of-doors. It is about bears. *Sigh.* Bears. And it says *bears* many times. As it is said, I quietly mouth the word, "bear." The program talks about the type and color of bears. Grizzly bears. That is the type of bear that raided the campsite the night of my stroke. There are black bears. They are smaller and the shape of their head is different. Either kind of bear can be dangerous. "— Bear. — Bear. — Bear."

Frank:
One night while Carol was in the hospital, I got there too late to get in through the normal entrance and had to go through the emergency room. I borrowed a dollar for a 7-Up since Carol had acquired a taste for ginger ale on the medevac flight from Fort Nelson. I got to her darkened room, not wanting to disturb her if she was asleep. Just as I pulled back the curtain to look into the room, her voice came out of the darkness with the same intonation I had been hearing for almost thirty years: "Well, hi there, Pard!" That was the first glimpse of the old personality that had been hidden beneath the confusion and fatigue of the stroke. It was a defining moment in the recovery process; now I knew that Carol was inside that stunned, tired body and that she would recover.

I just said a lot of words, didn't I? Yet, what did I say? Did it make sense? I said *Pard,* but what were the other words?

Why not the "bird" word?

One morning I stand by the window and gaze out over a thick hedge of flowered bouquets two deep the whole length of the windowsill. This morning it is not actively raining as it has been before. It is wet outside, but the haze is lifting and I can almost see the sunshine trying to pierce the clouds. More than that, I can see past the edge of the roof line below. In the distance I can see trees. Between the trees I see movement. The familiar movement of flying creatures. What is that word that names them? It escapes me. It escapes me as if I have never known it before.

"Bear?" I mouth out loud.

No, that is the word from the night before. Bears do not fly through the air.

I admire the bank of flowers on the windowsill. Flowers have never been more important. Since I cannot read, my eyes feast on the beauty of the flowers. Now, what is that word I am trying to remember? What is left of my brain thinks very hard. Very hard. *Ahhh, it is very close.* I try again.

"Bear?"

No, that is the same word I just tried and it was not right.

I watch some more. The flitting things are very far away. I cannot see them well enough to identify what kind they are. But I watch their flight. Some fly smoothly from place to place. Some hold out their wings and float on the wind. One swoops up with a rapid wing beat, then folds its wings and swoops down momentarily as if it is dive bombing. Up and down. Up and down. The pattern is repeated until it reaches its destination. The only word that comes is *bear*. But these cannot be bears.

I point out the window and ask the nurse, "h-Wat's that?"

"A tree?"

"No." I flap my arms to mimic the flitting thing.

"Bird?"

"Yes, — b – b — ird."

Bird. That is a short word and there is something about it that is similar to the bear word. Now I have another word to remember. *Bear* and

— and — ? ? ? — What is that word I just learned? The one that sounded like *bear* but whose creatures fly through the sky?

"— B – ear?"

No, that is the furry one.

"— Bear?"

No, that one has big teeth.

I think again; it seems so close. I whisper, "— Bear? — Bear?"

I've lost it. The nurse is gone and the word she gave me does not want to come back.

A speech therapist comes again. Good. But it is not the same lady who came before. That will be all right. She has my folder. This lady will know where to start teaching me words. This lady tries to carry on a conversation with me. She wants me to talk. I am pretty proud about the words I have learned since the stroke. I repeat to her Frank's story to me about the evacuation.

She listens. Then says, "I do not understand you." I am crushed. I have been happily jabbering nonsense and did not even know it. Well, at least that shows her I certainly need words. She has the result of the test from yesterday. She must be here to teach me words.

No, she is not ready to teach me. She comes to test me again. She repeats the same flash cards as the lady did before with the same results. Well, almost the same. I do manage to remember the word *car* under the picture of a car. I also remember to say *car* for a picture of a *chair* and any other word shown on the card that starts with a "c". So far, I am not impressed with speech therapy. You would think that if it is important for me to say the words on the cards, they would teach me how to say them and give me a way to remember them.

This day goes on. I lie in the bed hooked to the IV stand. I doze. I think. I stew. I walk over to the window. I watch the flying thing without a name. I try again, "Bear." No, that was the furry thing from last night. I take the IV stand with me and do another loop of the floor. I need to exercise. I need to get my strength back. Exercise takes me down the hallway to the interior court yard. There is one of those flying things down there. I watch it for a long time. My brain searches for its word.

There it is. It is very close in the front of my mouth. Thinking, thinking, thinking. Trying, trying, trying to put the shape in my mouth. There!

"— B – ear!"

Oh well.

The flying thing name did not stick in my brain. It was there. Now it is not. Without the word, my brain does not know how to shape my mouth to generate the word. I ponder. I look out the window into the court yard. Hospital employees come into the yard from a door below. They light up their cigarettes. *If you ever have a stroke, you will wish you never smoked. Just an aphasic stroke like mine and you will never work in the hospital again.*

One last look. "— B – b — ear! Bear!"

No.

Back to the room. Back to rest. Back to the dreadful blood draw basket. Out of bed to march in place, to swing my arm around to try to get my circulation going so she can find my vein. Susan says she thinks this is the last draw. Tomorrow I should be going home.

Home? Tomorrow? Yes! But? There are so many uncertainties. So many unknowns. So many questions to which the doctors have no answers. Will I ever talk? I mean really talk? Really read and write? And the blood clotting factor? Will I form more clots? Would surgical closure of the patent foramen ovale eliminate the risk of another stroke? There is a sense of euphoria at the prospect of going home and at the same time, one of fearfulness. Yet it is better to deal with that at home than it is here in the hospital.

Frank:

I started getting weepy in the ER, but held things in pretty well until the night before Carol was due back home. I broke down completely. I cried for an hour; the stress had been more intense than anything I had ever experienced in accidents in the woods or in Mountain Rescue. Hauling strangers or friends out of trouble is nothing like the experience of bringing your wounded life partner out of the wilds to a place where she could be helped.

I had lost sight of everything but the goal of getting Carol to the hospital. After the first prayers in the tent and in the van I stopped praying and simply fought to get her to aid before anything else went wrong in her brain. And yet, when Job lost his family, he was still able to say, "Jehovah himself has given, and Jehovah himself has taken away; let the name of Jehovah continue to be blessed." I have had to re-evaluate my spirituality, remembering that everything we have is on loan from our Creator.

As I am enjoying a good sleep my last night, a man comes into the room. He wants to talk to me about Coumadin. This is not a good time for him to come. It is late. It is dark outside. I have been asleep. My body is tired. My brain is on *off*. Even in the day time and rested I can barely process the English language. I am supposed to be alert now? I try to clear my head, sit up in the bed and turn on the light so I can watch and listen to what he says. I already know that Coumadin is warfarin and warfarin is rat poison. I know it makes rats and mice die because it causes them to bleed to death. So, whatever he can say to me will be important. I do not want to bleed to death. I try to listen. It would be nice if Frank were here to hear the words, too, so he could tell them to me again later. I only hope to learn enough from the man that I do not bleed to death.

Taking Coumadin is apparently more complicated than taking a pill a day. This pill depends. The pill depends on the dosage. The dosage depends on how much I weigh, how active I am, how many green vegetables I eat. Green vegetables make vitamin K. Vitamin K causes blood to coagulate. Coumadin counteracts that. He says it is all right for me to eat green vegetables, but I need to eat the same amount every day not to disrupt the Coumadin dosage. I am also supposed to maintain the same degree of exercise. Prescribed medication, vitamins and supplements can also influence the efficiency of the dosage.

Then he tells me the dosage is determined from blood tests. He uses new words. The blood sample finds my prothrombin time, protime, or PT. He also uses the word INR for international normalized ratio. The new words drain through my mind as through a sieve; as a teacher's words do not reach the mind of a day-dreaming student. But I am concentrating as hard as I can. I cannot dwell on the new words, or I will miss what he is going to say next. I try to learn what he keeps talking about. He says that after I go home, my doctor will test my protime every few days until the INR reaches the right level. Then he will test me every few weeks and, at the least, every month.

The man talks as if the Coumadin is safe. But his list of cautions denies that. He says I will not bleed to death from a cut. But it will take longer for the bleeding to stop. *Does he know how many sharp tools I use?* I should wear a medical alert bracelet in case I am in an accident. *Why do I need that if I am not going to bleed to death anyway?* I should tell my doctor if I change my exercise routine, or my diet, or my medications, or ... or ... so the doctor can check my protime more often to stabilize my dosage. So, while I do not remember the important words, I get the gist of it. I get the gist of it that it will be very difficult to live too far away from a doctor and a laboratory for any length of time. It will be difficult to take a long canoe trip in the Yukon. Dr. Braun says I should be on Coumadin no more than a year. A year! I can live with that but cannot imagine coping with Coumadin longer than that. I still want to go on longer canoe trips on the Yukon.

Sleep again. Then I am awakened by the bearer of a draw blood basket. "No!" I insist. "Ssss-usan — say — NO! — *No* more!"

"No, your doctor wants to get one more blood draw."

A weary body wakes up. I unwrap myself from the snarl of tubing and wiring attached to me. Get out of bed. Swing my arm around to get my circulation going so they can find a vein. Get back into bed and hope one poke will spurt blood into the vial without causing more bruising.

Near morning the night nurse awakens me again while checking my vitals. His name is Tim; the same as our youngest son. It says Timothy on his name card. I cannot say the name, but I recognize the letters being the same as Tim's. He looks at me very directly and said his shift will be over soon, but he wanted to say goodbye since I will be going home. *That is nice.*

Kindly he says, "I think you are very independent."

Thinking this compliment deserves the best response I can provide, I take time, think hard and say very carefully, "Yes — I — am."

Still caringly, he says, "And you have a supportive family."

"Yes — I — do."

"I think you will do fine."

I look at him with appreciation and wonder. This man does not know me, has been taking care of me for only a night or two yet takes the time to give me such sincere encouragement. I would like to tell him how much this means to me. To know that one person has confidence in me. To have one person say to me in my stage of uncertainty they believe there is a future for me. I would like to say a lot of words to him to express my thankfulness but can only end with a measured, deliberate, "Thank — you."

This is discharge day. Dr. Glenn and Dr. Braun come by to review my condition and give me discharge orders. Both doctors believe the DVT clot going through the PFO was instrumental in causing my stroke. I am to take my Coumadin, not to take aspirin, birth control pills, or estrogen. The issue of whether to close the PFO can be addressed later.

What shall I take instead of aspirin? I hold my head, moaning, as if it hurts. The doctor asks, "Do you want to know what to take for headaches?"

I nod.

His response is that I should use Tylenol. *Tylenol?* Tylenol has always been nothing compared to aspirin. I am going to miss my aspirin. One more reason to eliminate the Coumadin as soon as possible.

Dr. Braun (Neurologist):
When I first saw her in the hospital, her only positive findings were a marked expressive aphasia and a minimal right upper extremity drift. Within 12-18 hours, the drift disappeared and her aphasia improved.

Initially, we recommended a carotid Doppler, and this was unremarkable. Because of this, I asked that a TEE be done, and this was done by Dr. Malone who noted a fairly significant PFO. Because of this, a venous Doppler of the legs was done, and it did show a DVT. Based on this, it was recommended to start heparin and then switch her to Coumadin.

In summary, Ms Schultz has had a small stroke involving the language center causing an expressive aphasia. The etiology of the stroke is most likely due to an embolus from a DVT through the PFO. Less likely, it is related to migraine/BCP. At this point, I would recommend no BCP and no ergots. Further, I would recommend Coumadin for a minimum of one year.

Two big questions are: Does her PFO need to be done or corrected surgically. The other question is how long to treat with Coumadin. Her husband who is quite intelligent and well-informed is concerned about the long risks of Coumadin. He also notes that he would be worried about surgery for the PFO as she is a Jehovah's Witness and doesn't want a blood transfusion.

The final decision does not need to be made at this point. They are in agreement to treat with Coumadin for one year, and at that point, they want to decide whether or not to switch to aspirin. The decision on this is deferred to Dr. Glenn and Dr. Malone.

The IV is removed, the electrode patches pulled off. Frank has brought real clothes for me to wear for the trip home. We wait only for the discharge papers.

August 21, 1998
Dr. Glenn:
Activity as tolerated

Coumadin 5 mg every day. Follow instructions given by pharmacist.

Appointments:

OP PT Evaluation with Terry Busch, 2:30, Monday 8/24.

Lab draw (Protime) on Monday 8/24/98 at MOP.

OP Speech Therapy, 8/24, 10:30, South Campus Jersey St.

Glenn on Thur 8/27 at 11:30 am.

We are both happy. I am alive and we are going home.

Then at the last minute, another official looking lady with a briefcase comes into the room. She introduces herself as a speech therapist. *What? A third speech therapist? I did not know there could be so many of them. A lot of people must have aphasic strokes.* She tells me her name, and I immediately take hold of her name tag. I put on my reading glasses to look at her name tag as if that will say her name to me. She says her name again and I repeat it as I read her name tag. She says, "You may benefit from phonics."

Phonics. It echoes from the past. It echoes from learning to read when I was in elementary school. It echoes from when my boys were learning to read. At that time, there was a controversy about it. But phonics sounds good to me. I cannot remember the word, but I am happy that this speech therapist will use it with me.

The good happiness does not last long. This speech therapist is not here to teach me anything, either. There is more testing that does not teach me anything. All the same, I hope this lady will be the one who works with me when I start speech therapy next week.

Finally, we are really going home, and we are ready to ease out of the room toward the street below. However, none of this just walking out of the hospital. Here comes an escort with a wheelchair for me. *Oh well.* At least this time I am not loaded up with pain medication like I was after my appendectomy. The motion of the wheelchair should not make me nauseous this time. I should be able to get down to the curb without vomiting. What a mundane and unpleasant memory to occupy my thoughts when I should be feeling the release to freedom after being confined in the hospital for nearly a week! Maybe it is because I do not feel free in the true sense. I am still bound by wordlessness.

Part Three

Going Home

Unfamiliar familiarity

Stopping by our store, Base Camp, on the way home, Frank takes me inside so the staff can see me. Takes me inside so I can see that the store is still operating without me. It is wonderful to see the staff. Sheepishly, I smile to those who greet me. I say, "Hi."

Things that had been familiar are now strange to me. Walls hang with climbing equipment I had known how to describe. Racks display technical clothing useful first in function and then in fashion. I had known their construction and their fibers' characteristics and could have counseled a customer to their appropriate selection. Glass counters and shelves are full of camping accessories I had known words for and words to describe their virtues. The register? I had known what it was called and had been adept at working it. It was all strange now.

Frank leads me up the stairs to the office where Tom and Tim join us. This is the first stairway I have taken since my stroke. Somehow I do not have the strength I should have. My usual running up them is beyond me. The railing supports me, Frank at my side. My feet follow the treads up in a climber's rest step. Place one foot up; lift up one step. Pause. Next foot up. Lift up one next step. Pause. Repeat. Pause. Repeat. Pause. Into the office to collapse in a chair.

Do this

The office has not changed. Frank and the boys briefly talk business while I catch my breath and collect my thoughts. I cannot concentrate on what the guys are talking about and at the same time think about what I need to do. Their conversation passes over my head; I concentrate on the business I need to do before I go home. The boys need to know how to do what I usually do myself.

I open a drawer from the filing cabinet and look for the Washington State Department of Revenue folder. The title does not say words to me, but I recognize the folder in its customary place. I pull it out.

Frank tells me to stop working. It is too stressful for me. He threatens to take me right home. By action I object and insist. It will be more stressful for me not to show Tom the tax folder. It will be very stressful for me to not have the sales tax paid on time. There are repercussions if it is not done and paid on time. A penalty will cost us money.

I show Tom the folder. "Do this," I say, and show him on the calendar that it is due on the 25th. Then, I go to the Rolodex and rotate the wheel to the card that rolls up our bookkeeper's name and phone number. I show that to Tom. I look at the bookkeeper's name to try to say it to Tom. "G — w — en." Gwen will help Tom if he needs it. He understands and now he knows where to find her phone number. I know Tom will be able to master the sales tax form if he puts his mind to it.

Meanwhile Frank is worried about my exertion. He gathers me up and takes me home.

A lot has happened at home — a lot at home has not happened

There is a degree of tranquility in arriving home. The late August slanted sunshine barely reaches into our wooded clearing. Seen from the driveway, our log sauna welcomes me in the distance. When I get out of the car, it is a pleasant approaching-fall temperature. I breathe deeply. Then in turning to our home, I see it has not necessarily been a refuge of quiet tranquility. Those living here have not been living a normal life.

Tim has moved into our house with all his worldly possessions. There are piles on the porch and in the living room and in his old bedroom. While we were in the Yukon, Tim had been minding the store, guiding trips in the mountains, attending a trade show for us, and moving his dwelling place. Our house is his pausing spot between residences. It will be great to have Tim home with us for awhile. The piles represent his need to resolve his many unfinished tasks, and, to us, an urgency to achieve order.

It is also apparent that Frank had little time beyond taking care of me while I was in the hospital. A grocery bag full of mail and another pile on the counter want attention. Piles of newspapers want reading. The camping gear from the Yukon River canoe trip lies in piles. The tent and sleeping bags are spread out airing. The kitchen kit bags are in various degrees of being unpacked. All wait to be put away. Frank has been preoccupied. Overwhelmed. It is overwhelming to me, too, but I do not care. I cannot talk well, but I feel that with returning strength I will be able to slowly bring order to this disarray. At least I will be able to put things in their places. I do not know how I am going to manage the tasks that require speaking and reading.

On top of the pile of mail is the *Reader's Digest*. That brings memories of before I could read, but was old enough to walk to the end of the block. Mother would take the three of us to the corner drugstore. I would walk along; Betty Ann would totter holding my hand, and Mother would push Mary Jane in the black baby buggy with its bent wheel. There, Mother bought her *Reader's Digest*. It had a very distinct cover pattern, and in time, I was able to point it out to Mother. Soon, Mother would give me a dime to go to the store myself to purchase the *Reader's Digest*. How long before I was able to read the *Digest* myself? Perhaps somewhat by the fourth grade, but probably not well until the sixth grade. *Heck*. That is a long time to learn to read. Now, I have six weeks to regain 50% of my losses. Somehow, I must learn words. I set a goal that somehow, I will be able to read this issue of the *Reader's Digest* before the next one comes. That is in four weeks! I look at the calendar on the bulletin board and make a mental mark for that date.

Continuing through the pile, I sort. Though I do not know what the words are, I recognize from experience the appearance of the pattern on the envelope. And from that I understand what the contents imply. I have to separate the important mail from the mail that is not. If it looks like one we throw away, I open it and make a pile for Frank to read. I know I should not throw it away myself. It needs to be read by someone who can read so I do not make a mistake. If it only has the letters "F-r-a-n-k" on it, I know my husband will want to look at it personally. That goes in a pile by itself. A few are hand addressed letters or cards with letters to Carol or Frank and Carol. Those go in another pile. Frank will read them to me later.

Then, there are the important envelopes. They are the ones that must be paid. This one looks like it is the one that makes our lights turn on. This one is so we hear words coming over a cord. Another makes the heat warm up when we do not want to build a wood fire. Then there are the ones we pay for the use of those plastic cards. Those will be difficult because I have always read every line to make sure each purchase is ours. Now it will be up to Frank. Then there are the ones with numbers from the bank. I sense my mathematical use of numbers is intact. Yet when I open the statements I realize dealing with them will not be as easy as I hoped.

The problem is that there are so many words to tell me what to do with the numbers. In trying to reconcile the account there are words I need to know to be able to put the numbers in the right spot. I never realized there were so many words connected with those numbers.

Enter ending checking account balance from front of this statement	$_____
Add checking deposit made but not shown by bank	+_____
Subtotal	$_____
Enter total outstanding checks and other withdrawals	–_____
Account balance	= $_____

Too many words to process even if I knew the words. How will I be able to put the numbers and the words together? To make sense of them? I have taken my ability to reconcile a bank statement for granted. Now, I set the statements aside.

Everything waits

Seemingly, everything waits willingly except me. I want to learn words *now* although my speech lesson will not be until Monday. Between necessary naps I watch for words. I try to capture them. There are words all around me. Frank and Tim and visitors throw out words. Some of them are to me. Some are about me. Some are to each other. I listen with great concentration. But most of the words do not have a landing spot in the void my stroke has created. I cannot learn words and digest the conversation at the same time. Neither can I sort out more than one conversation at the same time. It is maddening. My brain works so slowly. Words spoken to me must come with warning. Otherwise I must ask for them to be repeated. "What?" I say. Then if the words come too quickly, I ask "Again?" Sometimes I hear all the words, but they may not register. Sometimes a word catches in the conversation because I do not understand it. When my brain does not make sense of a crucial word, time stops. My brain mulls over that one word to make sense of it. In the meantime, other people have kept on talking. My brain has missed the rest of the statement – so all the words are lost.

Then there is a problem with my mouth. It is one thing to think in my mind that I have learned what a word sounds like. It is another thing to make my mouth form the sounds. I try a sound. The sound is not right. I try again with my tongue and lips in a different position. Again I err. I say it differently. When someone is there with me, they will repeat the word for me. Somehow, when I hear the word is not sounded out correctly, I know to try again. When a word comes out correctly, I recognize it as a real word.

Writing? My hand copies words, but my head does not think up words. Reading? The words I see do not represent sounds, nor do they have meaning. Hearing? Why can I not remember words simply by listening to them? Why do I understand some words as they are spoken to me? And why do others get stuck in the middle of the stream of conversation in such a way that I do not understand them at all? Why do I have to listen so attentively?

How can I wonder about these things and have my brain be seeking solutions without having words to fuel the wondering? Seemingly, my first task is to learn words because without words, I cannot talk. I cannot read. I cannot write. It seems that if I can make words stick in my head, my head will also recognize those words when they are spoken to me. Then I will be able to understand what people are saying. Moreover, I ought to be able to retrieve them and spit them out at will.

How can I learn words **now** before we see the speech therapist on Monday? Frank and I try any way we can to make progress. We read. I am as a toddler sitting in a parent's lap being read to. Frank points out newspaper headlines to me and summarizes the articles to me. On Sunday we look at the comics. Garfield is the easiest one. I get the gist of the comic by looking at the illustrations because it is largely visual. Then Frank reads to me by pointing to the words. As time goes on, I can say some of the Garfield words myself. This is because, though I do not realize it, they are largely phonetic. "Ooof? Woof! Thump! HaHaHa! Bonk!"

There are some things I can do myself before I see the speech therapist. I write down my name until I can write it without looking at it on my driver's license. I practice saying my name. Not spontaneously.

It takes a lot of premeditated thinking. Each sound is thought about before I say it. "L–u — cy." That one is not easy. I have not used that name very much. It was my mother's name. I have always used the middle one, "—C — arol." And the last one; that is from my husband. "— Sssssh — ul — tz." The sounds that go along with the names do not all look like the letters ought to sound to me, but Frank says them to me, and I try to repeat them along with the written word.

I look at Frank's name on an envelope and write it down. I have to ask him to repeat his name many times before I can remember how to say *Frank*. Likewise with the names of our sons, Tom and Tim. Frank explains, "You can remember who is who because the 'o' in Tom is round like his head. The 'i' in Tim is long and narrow like his face." Then I practice saying their names.

Then there is our address, Chuckanut Drive. That is the name I thought was so funny at the hospital. I learn to write it by memory. The word is long. It is harder to remember how to say it. I try to remember it starts with the same "ch" sound as in *chocolate*, the word Irene taught me at the hospital. Why does my road name have to be so long? The city is long, too. Bellingham. And WA? I know that stands for a long name, but I do not know what it is much less how to spell it. Still, I practice to be able to write. I am glad to be able to have the use of my right hand, that the paralysis went away.

More I do not know

I learn more about what I do not know. Tom calls. I answer the phone. Frank is outside. Tom wants to leave a message for Frank. I cannot remember the words long enough to repeat the message. Neither can I write them down.

Tom says, "Mom, just write down the phone number and Dad can call me back."

"Okay," I say. I think that will be easy enough.

Tom says, "Six fifty, eighty one ninety"

"hh-Wat?"

Then Tom gives me one number at a time, "Six."

Searching, searching, searching. *Six, six, six?* There is no image in the empty spot in my head for the number *six*! After searching the empty spot, I guess and write down "7".

"Okay."

Tom says, "Five."

After another long searching pause to sort out the number, I write down "4".

"Okay."

Then, "Zero."

"Zee - ro?"

"Right, zero."

"hh-Wat's that?"

"Mom, it is a circle."

"C — ir — cle? — h-Wat's that?"

"It's the round number."

"Rrr — round?"

"Round. It has a hole in it."

"A — h-hole?"

"Round like a donut with a hole in it."

"Do — nut?"

"Mom, you know what a donut is. You eat it."

"Oooh, Okay."

"The number zero looks like a donut. It is a circle with a hole in the middle. It is also called an "o".

"Ahhh." I get the idea. I write down "0".

Next Tom says, "Eight."

Eight? What number is that? Again my mind searches all the empty crevasses within the sucking empty hole that is my brain. Looking,

looking, looking. And looking some more. I cannot place it. Eight does not match up with any number in my mind!

"Eight?" I ask.

"Eight is after seven."

"Af — ter?" I say to Tom.

Tom, by this time, realizes I am not going to be able to write down a phone number when he tells me one.

He says, "Mom, can you say your numbers?"

Exasperated, I spout out, "YES! – ONE – TWO – THREE – FOUR – FIVE – SIX – SEVEN – EIGHT – NINE – TEN!"

"Can you follow the numbers on the phone keyboard?"

"The key — board?"

"Yes, the keyboard. You know, the numbers on the phone."

"Ah-ha. Yes," I say.

"Okay, Mom, I am going to start saying the numbers at the top of the keyboard. You follow along and when I stop on a number, you write it down."

"Okay," I say. *This is going to work! Having kids is worth something!*

While I watch the buttons, Tom starts: "One – Two – Three – Four – Five – Six," and stops.

I look at the button and write down "6." We proceed until Frank comes in. With a sigh, I hand the phone to Frank saying, "Tom."

Learning is going to be more complicated than I thought. Life is not going to stand still long enough to accommodate the additional necessary steps I will need to function in a world of words. People are not going to stand still long enough to accommodate my deficiencies.

Along with learning about what I do not know, I also try to determine what I do know. I still enjoy music. Can I sing? Quietly I hum a tune, but the words do not come. I seem to be able to recite numbers by rote. But if I am interrupted in my counting, I do not know what the last number was. Even if I can still say the last number, I do not know what that number was. I have to start counting again. Obviously, I simply cannot understand a phone number given over the phone. What about my letters? I seem to be able to recite them, but, as with the numbers, if I am interrupted in the middle of the alphabet, I do not know where I am. Though I may say the letter in the middle of nowhere and listen to it myself, I do not know what letter I am saying. Each plus, it seems, has several minuses.

The first days at home are festive ones. Family and friends come by with encouragement, flowers and meals.

Frank:
So many people helped from the first panicky phone call. Friends cooked many meals for us in the first weeks when Carol couldn't cook, and I was overwhelmed by work and the need to care for her.

When I am tired, I nap. As a matter of fact, I need so many naps that it is arduous to climb up the stairs all the time to the bedroom. I try to nap on the couch, but it is not comfortable for my painful back. Frank clears a place on the living room floor and lays out a backpacking mattress. On that, my back is able to stretch out flat on a hard surface. It becomes my daytime nap pad.

Frank answers and fields phone calls from our out-of-town family and relays the conversations to me. And besides feeding words to me, he is also cooking, making sure I get my Coumadin, and starting a calendar for me. He takes me on short walks on the interurban trail. The days feel good. They feel like I will be gaining strength and will be on an upward trend toward good health and recovery.

Therapy day!

Monday comes with a full schedule. This is the speech therapy day. Then, is my pro-time blood draw and then a physical therapy evaluation. Frank and I are excited about the day's schedule. Frank will be my advocate, my spokesman, my driver, my companion.

Frank is not sure where to go for speech. Or at least he pretends he does not. He asks where we are going.

Lots of luck getting it from me. However, I have an idea of where we are going. I had looked over the discharge order several times trying to make sense of it.

OP Speech Therapy
8/24/1998 10:30
South Campus, Jersey St.

One word there was familiar to my eye. It was *Jersey*. I had been on Jersey Street before. From that street was the entrance to the St. Joseph Hospital South Campus Rehabilitation Center. So, here we go down Chuckanut toward town and then into town toward South Campus. Frank says to me, "Where are we going?"

Vaguely, imprinted somewhere in my head is the picture of *Jersey*. But it is very faint in my mind. I point the correct direction for Frank while I am trying to bring forth the *Jersey* sound word that fades in and out of my mind. Along with the *Jersey* word fade in and out the memories of living with the Larsen's.

—⁂—

The *Jersey* word comes from the Larsen farm in Ferndale when I first came to Whatcom County thirty years ago. I had been on a road trip from the Midwest in the fall of 1968 and was almost out of money. It was time to get a job or call Mother to have her transfer the emergency funds from my savings to my checking account and head back home to Indiana. I had camped at Birch Bay State Park. In the morning I drove east. It was a clear, crisp day with Mt. Baker gleaming over the horizon. It was farming country. A farm? I had never worked on a farm before. It might be a good experience. Maybe I could find work on a farm in exchange for room and board. I drove into the first farm driveway to inquire. The farmer there said he was retired and did not need help, but the Larsens over on the other side of the county block milked cows and had kids about my age.

As I drove up the driveway, Alice Larsen came from her house. I parked my VW Bug and walked up to her. I am sure I caught her off guard, but there was never a pause after I told her I would like to live on a farm for a while for room and board. Alice said, "I'm on my way to town. Get in the car and we'll talk about it."

Alice was a classic. We first went to a bar in the basement of a restaurant. I thought that was a peculiar place to visit so early in the morning. (Was she testing to see if I had a drinking problem?) "What would you like to drink," she said. "A beer?"

I did not drink so I had a Coke.

Meanwhile, Alice had to know everything about me. I was not sure about Alice, however. There was gruffness and a strange dry humor about her. She was definitely not the run-of-the-mill type of person. When we got back to the farm she said, "Come on in. I'll talk to Paul."

Alice and Paul took me in and treated me as part of the family. They offered a room upstairs, but I felt I was intruding enough. I declined the bed and accepted the hayloft. Alice made sure I wrote my mother. And then one day, I found, when I saw her coming from the mail box waving a letter, she had also written my mother.

Over the course of the next few weeks, Alice and Paul introduced me to dairying. I woke up in the hayloft every morning when Paul came in to curse at the cows and was on the floor by the time Alice got to the barn. "Grab the grain scoop and give that cow two scoops; that one another half a scoop. That's Bessie, that one is Rose. That one is milked separately. Its milk goes to the cats. Take the broom and sweep that out. Get the shovel. Shovel that out." Then Alice was back to the house to cook breakfast for us. Then she was out to work with the calves. Such dedication. Milk two times a day. Chores between milking. Cooking. No time for herself but she had time for me as a stranger off the road.

Alice had friends over to meet me. She sent me to a stock auction and took me to a farmers' meeting. At the farmers' meeting Alice introduced me to a couple who milked Jersey cows. She explained she and Paul milked Holsteins. Holsteins were the big black and white cows I saw on their farm. They produced large quantities of milk, but the milk was not as rich as Jersey milk. The Jersey cows, she said, were a much smaller, golden brown cow. They didn't produce as much milk, but the milk had a very high fat content. That's where cream and butter largely came from.

—⚉—

All these memories are flashing in and out of focus while I am being driven up Chestnut Street. Desperately, I am trying to remember any other word that might prompt Frank to think of the word *Jersey* for me. *Brown* comes into my imagination. But then only the color, not the letters of the word. I could say it makes cream. *Cream?* Again, I can only picture its color, its texture, its taste. I see in my mind the thick cream that was on the top of every glass milk bottle the milkman left in the milk-box on our front porch when I was a kid. My mother would pour it off to use with coffee or just shake it up with the milk in the bottom. Sometimes she would beat the cream to a mounded froth to put on pie. What was that called? These days we squirt the same stuff out of a can. What is that called? If I had that word, I could tell Frank that Jersey cows made whipping cream. Meanwhile, we are getting closer and closer to where I know Jersey Street will show up.

Then suddenly, "Cow!" comes out, "Cow."

Frank thinks I am out of my mind, which is true. I could not argue against it even if I could speak. Frank says, "Cow?"

"Cow. Go, cow." I point up the street over the dashboard indicating Frank should keep driving.

"We're going to South Campus," he says.

"Yes, 'cow,'" I keep saying and keep pointing straight.

I watch for the *Jersey* word on the street sign. It is coming soon. "There!" I say seeing the sign and point up to it for Frank to see it.

"Jersey Street, like Jersey cow," he says.

"Yes," I say a little indignant. Of course *cow* means *Jersey,* and, of course, it is relevant to our finding the right street. Frank should know that!

Frank slows the van to get ready to turn left onto Jersey Street, but I say, "No!" I know it is a one-way street against us. "There, there," I point straight with great exaggeration followed by more sweeping motions that we have to go around the campus and come back onto Jersey from the other direction.

Speech therapy

While Frank registers me at the counter, I look over the business card selection. I am looking for three business cards for the names of the three speech therapists who helped me at the hospital. Curiously, there is only one person's business card here that has the word *speech* on it. That does not explain why I have had three speech therapists so far. If three are not listed here, where did they come from? Which of the three is the Ms. Sally Sands (fictitious name), MA-CCC listed on the card? I hope she is the last speech therapist who worked with me at the hospital, the one who said I might benefit from the *phonics* word I do not remember. As a matter of fact, she was the only one suggesting I might be able to speak again.

Frank and I find seats in the waiting room. Frank finds a magazine and occupies himself reading. I try all the chairs in the room one after the other. None of them supports a bad back. I sit up very straight wishing my back pain would go away and wish I could read like Frank. It would distract me from the pain. All I can do is look around me and think. The top of the thinking list, of course, is wondering about this Ms. Sands. Who is she? Will I recognize her as one of the speech therapists from the hospital? She has so many initials behind her name I am sure she is quite accomplished. She will sit me down and explain the plan to me. She will say, "This is how learning language works. After an aphasic stroke, this is what you have to do to learn words again. This is the plan. First we will ... Second we will ... And then ..."

A woman calls my name, "Carol." She does not look like any of the speech therapists who worked with me before. This is another woman. She is very dressed up. Overly-dressed up in my estimation. She looks like she spends most of her time indoors confined to a desk. She must really love teaching people how to talk to give up time in the out-of-doors. She is pleasant enough. I come forward. She says, "I'm Ms. Sands, your speech therapist. Follow me."

Frank introduces himself and asks if he can come along.

"By all means," she says. We follow the new speech therapist who is holding my old folder created by three other therapists. One plus three is four. This lady is the number four speech therapist in less than a week.

The classroom is a small office. There are shelves full of books and materials on one side. There is a small table big enough for Ms. Sands on one side and for me on the other. Again, the chair is not too comfortable. On the right side of the table against the wall is a window that opens into the hallway. It is one of those windows that allow people to watch me from the other side while I cannot see them. I wonder who is going to watch me.

Evidently, family members are welcome but not expected. Frank's feet are weary of standing so he sits on a counter. Ms. Sands notices and goes for a chair for him.

She wants to know more about me, not much of which I am able to tell her. Frank talks for me, answers Ms. Sands' questions about me. She asks, "Are you ready to learn?"

"Yes, yes, yes, work, work, work," I answer. Then there is a very peculiar lesson. Ms. Sands presents to me an illustration that looks like a coloring book page. There is a picture of a house and garage, a dog, some bushes, a ladder, a sidewalk in front of the house and up to the front door. There is a man and a boy. Then she asks me to tell her what I see.

I look and look. I know what those things are, but I do not have words for them. *Shoot, is she not going to teach me anything?* Seeing no response from me, she then asks me to point to the different things in the picture as she names them. I point to the first or second correctly, but then she talks too fast. She does not give my brain long enough to process her demands. When I point, she is three words ahead. So, of course, what I point to is not in synch with the word she gives.

Obviously, she is not teaching; she is testing. Again. I am being tested again! But she is smart. She has lots of initials behind her name. She will teach me these words. I really do want to know these words. They are common ones that will be useful to say. Certainly, she will write down the words on the page and let me take the coloring page home with me so I can learn them. Frank will help me learn them.

Initial Speech Language Evaluation and Treatment Plan
Ms. Sally Sands, MA-CCC, Speech Language Pathologist:

Speech Language Diagnosis: Aphasia

Significant Objective Findings: Patient is a 53 year old active woman. Presents with moderate receptive and expressive aphasia across all areas. Ms. Shultz has marked difficulty following two step directions and answering non-personal yes/no questions. Ms. Shultz is able to speak in very short phrases with many apraxic speech errors. Reading is limited to short two or three word phrases. Writing is limited to her name and address and some single word productions.

The page goes back in the folder. We do not get to take it home with us. Time is up and Frank and I are led down the hallway to schedule the next speech therapy appointment. I have not learned anything from a speech therapist yet in four sessions. I am not getting my money's worth. I can only hope that real teaching will start in the next session.

Hamburgers? Where are the hamburgers?

Hamburgers? Where are the hamburgers? I look and look. I ask Frank, "hh-Wat — I like?" We are at Dairy Queen. I am looking forward to having a hamburger here. It is one of my favorite places for a quick meal. I am so familiar with everything about it; I felt I would have no problem making myself at home here. Now I cannot find *hamburger.*

Frank asks, "Hamburgers?"

Yes, I know that. My stroke had taken the word. "Yes, h-ham — b-burgers." Still, I keep looking. I cannot find *hamburger* on the menu board. "Hamburger." I do not know how to spell it but I have spent so much time eating at this Dairy Queen, I think I should be able to recognize *hamburger* on the menu. There was one hamburger I liked the best. I was looking for it hoping it would help me say the type of hamburger I liked so Frank could order for me. *Hamburger, hamburger.* My eye, with stalls and starts, slowly scans the menu columns. No, it should be on the first column, but I do not recognize *hamburger* at all. Have they stopped serving hamburgers?

"Frank, no 'h-ham — b-burgers'. I — ka – ka – kan — not — find — ha-HAM — BURG – er."

"There they are," he says, pointing to the board where I thought they should have been.

"No — no — h-ham — burg – er."

"Carol, there they are. They say burgers."

Ohhh Shoot! I think while laughing, "Oh — b – burg — ers!" *So much to learn!*

"There — b-b – burg — er." While pointing down the list. "There, — one – two – three."

"The third one?" Frank asks.

"Yes — th – three."

"Does that mean you want the deluxe burger?"

"Yes — a – gain?"

"Deluxe burger?"

"Yes — Dee — Luxe."

Deluxe Burger. Deluxe Burger. I look at the print on the board. I mouth the sounds again quietly. I try to make a mental image of the words *Deluxe Burger* in my mind so I can remember them in my head, so I can say them again. *Deluxe Burger.* I also look at its position on the board so I can find it the next time.

Lab draw (Protime)

For some reason, we do not have to be on time for the protime. I have not gone to a doctor's office and not had to be on time. Frank takes us to the receiving counter. He gives the people behind the counter there my name. Shuffle, shuffle behind the counter and into folder shelves and cubby stashes. "Date of birth?"

Frank tells them.

"Oh." That folder goes away. Shuffle, shuffle to a different folder to find the right Carol Schultz.

It is a good thing Frank is listening because I have already found a seat in Dr. Glenn's office. I did not understand I was supposed to go to the lab. Neither did I understand the directions to get there. Frank leads me through another group's office, across a hallway to a small waiting room. "Here, here's the lab. Here's the lab paperwork. I'll be back."

On the left is a sliding window. I give the lab paperwork to a lady there and find a seat in the waiting room. The room is almost empty. I expect this will not take too long. Other people waiting in the room are called for their lab tests. In the meantime, more people come into the room and find seats. They are served. I wait. More come in. I wait. My eyes meet the eyes of the woman who comes in calling names. But she never calls my name. I wait some more. It has been a long day already with no naps and I am getting very tired. No longer able to keep my head up, I lay down on the couch to doze and rest. Frank comes back and sits down in the room with me. Sometimes, it seems I am the only patient in the room. The woman who keeps calling names notices me there but never calls my name. She has my paperwork. Why am I not called? I know we have another appointment, and we will miss it if I have to wait too much longer. Finally, after the woman took in a person before they could be seated, I muster up an attempt to tell Frank, "— They — af-ter — me."

Frank goes to the sliding window and talks to the woman. He asks why I have not been served. There is talk. Then he turns to me and asks if I have the paperwork.

I shake my head, "No", and point into the room beyond the sliding window. "There. — They — have."

"My wife says she left the paperwork with you."

Shuffle, shuffle. "Oh, here it is. Did she sign-in?"

Frank turns to me, "Did you sign-in?"

"h-Wat?" I say. *What sign-in?*

Frank turns to the woman and asks her about the sign-in.

She hands a clipboard to Frank as if to say to him, "Look, right here. Can't you see the sign-in sheet?" The inference is, "Can't your wife read?"

I cannot read. Neither did you point out the sign-in sheet when I gave you the lab work! What kind of operation is this?

The protime lab woman is not much more competent than the woman who took my paperwork. Protime becomes a bad word linked to all the poor blood draws I am experiencing. As we leave the lab, I question the quality of medical service for those who cannot read and cannot speak.

OT PT Evaluation

Frank:
Once Carol got home after her week in the hospital, we began putting things back together. I was the driver and go-fer just as she had been for me with my broken heels six years before. One of the first stops was at NW Physical Therapy. Terry Busch would evaluate Carol's physical condition and assess the need for physical therapy to recover from the stroke.

This office is more welcoming and accommodating than the lab, but the floor is still the most comfortable seat. However, this is familiar territory. Many of the staff here know Frank from the months he spent as a client here in 1992. Frank had fallen 30 feet onto concrete in an indoor climbing gym, shattering both heels. Two surgeries with two plates and 22 screws left him to heal for three months in a wheelchair. In those three months, I became the wheelchair fold-and-stow champion while Frank spent many hours with Terry in his rehabilitation physical therapy gym. Now, Frank is taking care of me and I am the patient. Fortunately, I am here only for an evaluation.

Terry's task is to determine whether the stroke has caused any physical damage. He takes me from a table, to the wall, to the floor having me move through various motions. He is intent on examining every conceivable motion a body can make. Things go smoothly until he gives me only verbal instructions. It is very confusing to sort out the differences between parts of the body and the directions he asks me to move. Terry has to show me the body part he is talking about. On the floor, he wants me to go through various patterns. "Go forward placing one foot in front of the other." *Too many words.* He has to show me what he wants me to do. Once he sets an example, I am able to copy. But to perform from verbal instruction alone is beyond me.

Frank:
After checking coordination, strength, and asking questions, Terry pronounced Carol completely without deficit physically. That was a real boost for our morale.

"Can Carol drive?" Frank asks. Terry says physically there should be no problem; I should ask my family doctor to see what he says.

Part Four

Running the Medical Gauntlet

Distrust

I am now one of the one-in-250 Americans affected by aphasia (National Aphasia Association, NAA). I have escaped being one of the 20% of stroke victims who die in the hospital (Cedars-Sinai Stroke Center). Now, I must escape being one of the 23% who have a recurrence in the first year (American Heart Association). My doctors are my lifeline, and I depend on them. How is it then I feel like I am running a gauntlet with those in the medical community?

Part of the problem is that my aphasia limits my communication with them. Secondly, they do not know how to communicate with me. While one million people in the United States suffer from aphasia, most people have never heard of it (NAA). Many of those in the medical community must be among them; they do not know the aphasic mind well enough to accommodate an aphasic's special needs. Additionally, it becomes apparent that the economic climate has forced them to minimize the time they spend with patients. They need to *hurry* while my aphasic brain works slowly.

I had trusted doctors until some years earlier when a surgeon told me to ignore a post-op finger surgery infection – to just double up on my pain medication. The resultant loss and grief cost me sorely. Since that time I had been, sadly, more skeptical. Now that I am aphasic, I am even more on edge in a doctor's office. Without speaking, I cannot express myself. My initial experience in the protime lab has not helped.

Not a clue

Two days after the protime, I am sleeping deeply, alone in the house. The phone rings. After finally hearing it ring through a sludgy mind, I wake up. I reach for the phone across the bed trying to remember where I am. What time of the day is it? All the good words I had practiced the day before have vanished overnight. My mouth is reluctant to articulate. Neither is my mind accepting words over the phone.

A woman's voice says rapidly, "Carolschultz?isthiscarolschultz?"

I hesitate in a stupor. I tell my mind to think, think as hard as it can. My mouth scrunches around inside trying to find just one word that will answer all her questions. *I do not understand you. Slow down.* But I do not have that many words. *I am not sure you want me.* That is too many words, too. To produce just one word takes all my concentration. "H-h-h-hoo?"

"Carolschultz?thisisdebbieatdoctorsmithsoffice."

How can I tell her to slow down? I do not know the *slow down* words. Now I recognize my name in her patter, but I think she has the wrong person. What else was in that long, fast line of sounds? Doctor? Doctor. She must be calling from a doctor's office. It does not seem like it is my doctor, though. I do not know a Debbie at Dr. Glenn's office. I am about to dismiss this rattling woman because she is not talking about my doctor. She must want the other Carol Schultz who is a patient in that practice and whose chart is often confused with mine. I am about to hang up when she prattles on.

"Thisisaboutyourprotime."

Protime, protime? Oh, protime. "Oh, okay," but I am confused about why Dr. Glenn's nurse is not calling me. I do not know this nurse or the doctor she mentions. Maybe that name is of another doctor in the group.

"Yourprotimeisthirtysevenpointtwoandyourinristhreepointthree thatistoohigh andyourdoctorwantsyoutoreduceyourcoumadindosag- etoonehalftablet thursdaythroughsaturdayand oneonsunday."

The sounds INR (international normalized ratio) catch my attention. What is it? Where does it fit? *Oh, it goes with the protime. It is the initials for long words that I do not remember the letters of.* "h - h - h – h-Wa — hWat?!" I say.

"Yesstarttaking twopointfivemiligramsstartingtomorrow andfivemi- lligramsonsunday."

Really, she must have my chart in her hand. Can she not read it? Does it not have a big red sticker on the front that declares:

Aphasic stroke patient:
- That means she does not speak well and probably does not understand you either.
- Talk slowly in short phrases.
- Give the patient time to respond to you; be sure she understands you.

This nurse does not have a clue. I know it is important to know what my INR time is and to change my Coumadin dosage as prescribed. To her, I say, "I am slow. Again. — t — t-Tell me again." I must concentrate very hard this time to pick up the dosages correctly.

"Wellthatsokiseethedoctor willseeyoutomorrowthedoctor willtalk-toyou aboutit."

Click.

Unfortunately, this is typical of my experience at Dr. Glenn's office. Sometimes his staff calls and leaves a message. Would I please call back? But they never leave the recommended Coumadin dosages on the message machine so I can have Frank translate it for me. That does not make sense to me. Why cannot the personnel of a doctor's office with all their years of education figure that out?

For me to return the call is in vain. I cannot understand recorded answering machine prompts. Even if a real person answers, I need to have Frank speak for me. Worse, if Frank does call, they will not talk to him. It is a violation of federal law for Frank to speak for me, to get my dosages. Yet, how am I to obtain the information?

In the meantime, my health is deteriorating. It is alarming to me because I was feeling so well coming out of the hospital. One week of healing and gaining strength at home and I am in a downhill spiral. Whereas before I could sleep all night and take deep naps at will, now I do not sleep at all. At first I think it is the mattress. I move into one of the boys' old rooms and try to sleep in a newer twin bed mattress. Still, I am kept awake thinking, thinking without words. I try to find the words for what I am thinking until an uncomfortable build-up of urine in my bladder forces me to the bathroom. Forty minutes to an hour between bathroom stops, but still no sleep.

When I try to take a nap during the day, my heart throbs heavily and rapidly. My body seems to shake. Pound, pound, pound preventing me from sleeping. I am so tired my brain resists learning the words I so desperately need. Not only am I weary, but I have no physical strength. I am always out of breath. Sweat exudes from my body for no apparent reason. At night, I cannot stand to lie next to my husband. The covers are too hot. I wake up to go to the bathroom at night and find my sleep shirt and the sheets are soaked. Also, headaches, blurred vision, light-headedness.

I can only blame this ill health on the Coumadin. It is the only variable introduced to my life since my stroke. Painfully, I spend hours deciphering half of a very small page from the Coumadin guide. At the top of the page is "Call your healthcare provider right away if you have … headache, dizziness, trouble breathing, chest pain, or if you feel weak or more tired than usual." That fits my symptoms. It's the Coumadin for sure. It is the Coumadin and I am not able to stabilize it. Protimes every few days do not keep it in the recommended range and the doctor's office does not communicate with me in a timely manner.

And though Frank and I find Dr. Glenn sincere, he does not agree the Coumadin is the problem. He prescribes a high blood pressure drug.

I have never had high blood pressure before. How do you explain that I have it now so suddenly?

He suggests I should try Tylenol PM for sleeping. He has prescribed a FSH (follitropin) test that shows I am probably in pre-menopause.

I would guess so – or beyond – since my last period was nonexistent. But why don't you ask me?

Then he says a hormone replacement therapy might help my hot flashes. But since he and Dr. Braun both agree I should not use any estrogen products, he could prescribe a different hormone. That sounds good to me. I am anxious to get rid of these paralyzing episodes of hotness.

That satisfies me until I get home with the newly prescribed bottle of medroxyprogesterone, known by its brand name, Provera. With the prescription from the pharmacist comes the information sheet. At this time, I still cannot really read but by taking a lot of time, I am able to find the *Precautions* and *Drug Interactions* words. Some of the words I recognize and though I cannot say them, I do not like them. I pick out; *high blood pressure...migraine headaches...strokes...blood clots.* "Medroxyprogesterone may slightly increase your risk of stroke, blood clots, high blood pressure."

I have had a stroke. I have had blood clots. I have had migraines. I am on high blood pressure medication now. What is he thinking of?

I highlight the culprit words with yellow highlighter. I show it to Frank. "Look," I say. "Look. — No good. — See, bad."

Frank looks at the material, too, saying he agrees. It is bad.

"I — do not — want — to take."

Frank agrees, I should not take it.

Changing doctors

Our retired doctor friend, John Arnold, thinks I might be having clots in my lungs and recommends we see a pulmonary doctor. Frank understands that once I change by going to this new doctor, I will have to sever my association with Dr. Glenn. I do not really understand how this has to be the case, but I do not really care. I am fed up with Glenn's office. It has been several days since my last protime, and I have not heard from his office although Frank has inquired several times. Besides, I am feeling worse the whole time. Furthermore, his prescription of medroxyprogesterone has caused me to be less confident in him.

Frank:
We were walking a tightrope with the Coumadin: too little, and she could have a stroke from a clot; too much, and she stood a chance of a hemorrhage in the brain or serious bleeding from a slight cut. We went six days after her blood draw once, without knowing what her clotting time was because the nurse would not give me the information over the phone. When we finally found the protime, it was far above the zone where we were supposed to keep it. We switched doctors then, not because of any problem with the doctor, but because of office politics and lack of timely notice.

Dr. Reilly (fictitious name), the pulmonary specialist, is on duty in the hospital. We meet him in the ER. It has been five weeks since I left the hospital. With an accusative attitude not typical of a professional, he wants to know, "Why are you here?"

Heck, I do not know. Someone ought to have been able to help me without putting me in the ER. If my own doctor could be reached past his front desk sentinels, I would probably not be here in the ER. Frank and John put me here and arranged for you to take care of me. Can't you look at me and see I am not well and I do not talk well?

I'm pretty proud of the words I have acquired in five weeks, but there are still too few to carry on a conversation. I am frustrated at not having words. I am frustrated and angry that this doctor has a confrontational demeanor. This all builds up and I spurt out shouting, ***"I am tired of being tired all the time!"***

Frank is my spokesman. He gives the doctor a brief summary of my stroke and my history since. I think Dr. Reilly has not looked up my medical history and may not have realized I am aphasic. Frank explains to Dr. Reilly the experiences we have had not being able to get my INR from our family doctor and how our doctor friend, John, thinks my rapid pulse rate and shortness of breath may be evidence of a pulmonary embolism.

Dr. Reilly prescribes a series of tests to determine the cause of my symptoms. In spite of my original impression of him, he is thorough. He asks for blood chemistry in about as many ways as possible, including another protime. There are more chest x-rays and an EKG (electrocardiogram). While some results are pending analysis, Dr. Reilly did find my INR (international normalized ratio) to be 3.6. My recommended therapeutic level is 2.5, so he reduces my Coumadin dosage and asks me to get a protime in his office in two days. He keeps me on the blood pressure drug and increases it a bit. He also asks me to schedule a stress echo treadmill cardiogram. He wants to see me in a week or two when all the reports are in.

The next day we receive a call from Dr. Glenn's office with the INR report from my protime in his lab six days ago. It was 3.4, too high even then.

The price of independence

Up to this time, Frank or friends have driven me everywhere I have needed to go. Also, I have needed Frank with me at my doctor's appointments to help translate for me, to translate my questions for the doctor and translate to me what the doctors have said. He makes notes so we have a record of the conversations in a doctor's office since I would often get only the drift of what the doctor was talking about. With Frank's notes, we are able to go over them again when we go home. It has also been Frank's responsibility to make all my over-the-phone appointments since my brain does still not compute over the phone. I depend on my husband, but it is not fair to expect him to be there with me all the time.

Now that I am able to drive again, I feel like a kindergarten kid on the first day of school. I am old enough to go to school, and should be able to surmount the challenge of separation from home, but really still need my Mommy. Over the last few weeks I have felt I should be starting to lessen my dependence on Frank so he can go back to his place at the store. I know that when he is not there, we have to hire someone else to be in his place. And now that I am not helping, I know we are also paying someone else to take my place. One of the things I can do to ease the financial end of things is to start doing some of the errands, including some of my own appointments.

I point to the calendar where I have copied very neatly, from Frank's notes, the essence of the appointment.

8:30 Medical Group Suite "A" for new patients form

I also know the reason I am going is to have a blood draw for my protime. I ask Frank, "I drive?"

"Do you think you are up to it?"

Dr. Glenn said I could drive after a month, so it is time. "I think so."

As we go out to the vehicles, I think Frank will come with me in the passenger side, ready to coach me or take over if it seems I do not drive well. But no, he says he will watch, following me from behind. He will drive the pickup while I drive the van.

"Do you know how to get to Medical Group?"

"I think so." I cannot remember how I know it. I must have been there before. Maybe with Frank.

Operating a car is strange for the first time after several weeks of not driving at all. I am on visual autopilot. I suppose we are usually on visual autopilot after we become so familiar with an area we no longer need the names of streets and business names – no longer need the prompt from the signs, their printed words. Nevertheless, it is strange not to be able to read road signs quickly enough. They are gone too soon to comprehend them.

When we get to Medical Group I find a parking place and walk to the entrance expecting Frank to meet me there to go inside. Instead, Frank drives up in the pickup rolling down the window saying, "I'll go on to work," and drives away.

Well, that is not exactly what I expected. I thought Frank would be at my side. Well, I am a big girl. I'll manage.

This is an example of the misunderstanding that comes with aphasia. Later, I learned Frank had expected to take me and be there with me, as I assumed he would be. But when I wanted to drive, he thought I also wanted to take care of myself at the doctor's office.

Digging into my purse, I look for the notes on my pocket calendar. Suite A. I look for an "A". This facility is peculiar for a doctor's office. There is no office. Each doctors' group has a U-shaped counter extending into the hallway. The hallway has groups of chairs in it. Apparently, the hallway is the reception center and the waiting room for all the doctors. It is not very friendly. Definitely not cozy or inviting. I approach the counter, not sure about what I am to do. There are a lot of patients standing around the counter waiting to be served. I am impressed that so many of them are old people and seemingly in poor health. Some of them can barely stand up long enough to be served at the high counter. It would be nice if they could rest on a stool by the counter. They put their elbows on the counter and lean on them heavily. Obviously, Dr. Reilly's group serves very sick, old patients. Am I one of them? I, too, am becoming weary of standing, and I join the others allowing the counter to support me by my elbows.

Peeking over the counter, I see an assortment of computer monitors and keyboards. They are manned by people who more often than not have ear phones plugged to their heads. I wonder who they are listening to. Or if they are listening to anyone? They are not typing as if they are entering information. They are not talking through a little speaker as if they are on the phone with anyone. Neither are they taking care of the patients. What are they doing? Another thing that impresses me is that the work area is much too small. There are four stations in the U-shaped counter, but the women are so large only two women fit there comfortably. If one of them stands in the doorway behind the counter, no one else can pass until she moves.

Finally it is my turn. I am not sure where to start, nor the words to say them. "I am Carol Schultz." That should do it. She should be able to pull up the order to see why I am here.

Carol Schultz does not work. I say, "I am — L — Carol Schultz."

She gazes at her screen for a long time and wiggles her mouse. "No, you are not a patient here. Who is your doctor?"

Who is my doctor? I think uncomfortably while the lady waits uncomfortably. I look on the wall where the doctors' names are listed. I look for one that might be familiar. *Ahhh, there it is. Reilly. That's the one.* I look at the letters on that name. The lady is becoming impatient with me, but I am hurrying as fast as I can. I look at each letter and try to imagine how it will shape the sound in my mouth. "R". I will try that like the name of the letter, "ar". Next, "e". That says "e". Will it sound like its name? Long "e"? Store that away. The "i" letter says "i". Will it sound like a long "i"? I will try it. Two "l's". I will say it as one "el". Finally, "y". Will it make its own name "wi"? Mentally, I try saying the word using the names of the letters. "aR - e - i - el - wi"? No, that did not work. I must try to use Tim's consonant key to produce the consonant sounds. (See *Part Five, Quest for Words, Consonants.*) Oh, "r" as in *Rogers.* /r/. Oh, and "y" is at the end. Maybe it says "e". Meanwhile the lady is waiting. Still looking at the name placard, I start, "/R/ - e-i - el - e".

"Doctor Reilly?"

"Yes, R - i - ly. — I saw him — in the hos - pi - tal."

"You are not a patient here. Are you to see him today?"

"Baa - l - uu-d," I say while poking my arm at a blood draw needle site.

"A blood draw?"

"Yes."

She looks further for some record that I exist. Looking away from the computer screen, she speaks to another lady and goes through the too small door into the mysterious rooms behind. Coming back, she has a slip of paper and reaches for a clipboard with papers on it. "Here it is. Doctor Reilly hadn't entered you yet. Could I see your insurance card?" Giving me the clipboard and a pen, she says, "Fill out the new patient forms here, and then bring it back to me. Thenyouwillgototheprotimelabclinicdownthere."

Hesitantly, I take the clipboard with me and find a seat. *Can I do this?* I take a long time filling out the form to put my name in the right places and deciphering each word until the mental sounds make some sort of familiar word. Each word comes, painfully. Then I go over the phrases again to make sense of the sentences. Equally difficult is to find the words to write down. Fortunately, the words I need are very familiar personal ones often recorded in my purse. I hope I put the words in the right places.

A woman at the counter takes the clipboard and hands me a slip of paper with directions to, "Goondownthehallwaytotheprotimeclinic."

Argh. They have their words all memorized, and they say them so often they can hardly wait to get them out of their mouths. Too fast – too fast for me. She has waved her hand down the hallway toward that place I am supposed to go so I look down the hall to see if I can see a sign that will remind me of the words she said. Looking down the hallway, I do not see a sign that seems like it would be the right place. I turn back to the counter and find that the lady who had helped me is no longer there. There is still another woman at her computer. I move to stand in her line of sight so she will see me to know I need help. She knows I am there, but she does not acknowledge my presence. She steadily looks into her computer screen. She does not say anything to anyone who might be talking to her in her head piece. But still she stares attentively into the monitor.

I ask, "Can you — help me?"

After another period of silence, she turns her head to me, "Yes?"

"Where?" showing her the slip of paper.

"Ohgodownto theprotimelabonthelefthand sideofthehallway," pointing down the hallway."

"The what?"

"The protime lab. There will be a sign. You will find it."

Okay, Okay, the lab. I can find the lab. That is where they poke needles. "Thank you," and I head down the hallway. I watch for a lab sign all the way down the hallway to the end. No, not there. Going back down the hallway I look at every sign, and if there is a glass window on the door, I look inside to see if it looks like a lab. Finally, a door with a window in it. Looking into the room, I see another counter. I look at all the letters by the door. *Ahhh, Laboratory. Shoot! Lab is the beginning of the <u>lab</u>-o-r-a-t-o-r-y letters. How could I miss it?* I go in to the counter and wait until someone comes to the sliding glass doors.

"Your name," she asks.

"Carol Schultz, — L Carol Schultz."

"I don't see it here."

I give her the slip of paper.

"Oh, you need the protime lab. It is next door."

"Next door?" I am very confused by now. "Next door" is a new concept for me. "Next door?"

The poor lady thinks I have lost my senses. She says, "Next door. Go out down the hallway (waving her hand in the direction I am to go), and it is the next door."

Dutifully I go out down the hallway in the direction she has pointed. At the next door I expect to see a protime lab similar to Dr. Glenn's, but this room is the size of a closet. There is a desk in there but not a person. This cannot be a lab. It must be the janitor's work space.

Next door? What can they mean? If it is not the next door, what does it mean? Maybe it is *next door* as in next door *neighbor*. Maybe the protime is next door in a different building. I do not remember that there is another building in that direction. I think there was an empty field. But maybe there is one I did not notice when I drove by. I walk down the hallway past the other doctors' U-shaped reception counters until I get to the end of the building. There is a glass door there that goes outside, but it does not look like it is used. For all I know, the sign says *Emergency Exit Only,* and the door might make a racket if I open it. I look for a next door building past the glass door, but there is none. There is only an empty field. I walk back to the laboratory. When I get the lady's attention, I ask her again, "Where?" showing her my slip.

"The Protime Clinic. It's next door. It's the *next* door!"

I am near tears. "— I looked; — is it — out — side?"

Clearly the lady is exasperated with me and beyond helping me further. A patient waiting in the waiting room has watched the difficulties I am having and says to me, "I know where the Protime Clinic is. I will take you." I follow her out the door down the hallway about 10 feet where she shows me the door to the Protime Clinic. It is the janitor's closet. "Here it is." In the hallway she shows me a small-table with a box with cards in it. She says, "Take a number from the cards here, and take a seat. The nurse will help you."

"Thank — you," I say gratefully.

Clearly, I have needed my husband with me. I will have to ask him to come with me in the future.

We sit around in the hallway waiting for the nurse to call our numbers. A few seem to be younger than I am. One is in a wheelchair, another with an oxygen tank. Most look old and very sick. I do not feel that sick and I am not as old. I had a stroke, that is all, and I cannot talk.

When the nurse calls my name from the clinic door she ushers me into the "janitor's closet"! The nurse is organized, however. There is an index card file with all her patients' names in it. There is a reference chart from which she gauges the INR times against the recommended anticoagulation targets.

So, where is the blood draw basket? This does not look like a blood draw lab.

She takes my slip and makes out an index card for me. From the desk drawer below, she brings out an alcohol wipe, a Band-Aid, a lancet and a small piece of paper. She takes my finger, wipes it with the alcohol and pokes it with the lancet. Then she turns my finger over and squeezes a drop of blood onto the special paper. From that she slides the paper with the drop of blood into a little slot in a very small box. She makes small talk and puts the Band-Aid on the stab site while the machine hums – until its reader screen lights up with my INR and protime.

"Shoot. — Is that — all?" I say to the nurse.

"Yes, that is all there is." Then she pulls out a business card size card and writes down for me the next recommended Coumadin dosages. She also makes my next appointment and writes that down. I have all the information I need in a few minutes and no blood draw needles stabbing around in my arm. I have all the information I need to monitor my anticoagulation without having to coax and beg for several days to get the information out of Dr. Glenn's office. This is swell! This alone makes changing doctors worthwhile.

Shoot! This will help. This too-small-to-be-a-lab janitor's closet is big enough!

Frank:
At the new practice, Carol could get a finger stick test, and have the results in ten minutes. These really helped her peace of mind, and let us focus on the larger issues.

Confidence issues

Dr. Reilly is a young doctor. I think this is his first position as a practicing doctor out of residency. His specialty is pulmonary medicine, but his certificate also says he is an internal medical doctor. Dr. Reilly takes my care seriously, and reaches beyond his specialty to bring in advice from others in his group to know how to treat me. In spite of that, there is often conflict between us.

I do not want to keep taking Coumadin more than a year. Dr. Braun told us there is a 5% risk of a major bleeding episode each year from using therapeutic dosages of Coumadin. He said that was cumulative so in 20 years there was a 100% chance of a major bleeding complication. That was why he was interested in having me off Coumadin after a year. I agreed. I expected to live longer than twenty years. I was, also, beginning to see that it would be very complicated for me to be able to be away from a blood lab for more than a few days if I were on Coumadin. I wanted to be off it as soon as possible.

Dr. Reilly, in an early appointment, emphasized he wanted me to be on Coumadin the rest of my life. "I'm trying to prevent you from having another stroke," he said. "You don't want to close your PFO surgically because you are a Jehovah's Witness and you won't take blood. Therefore, you will be on Coumadin forever."

In the first place, you do not know what I think. Secondly, you do not know what you are talking about. You do not know about Jehovah's Witnesses or about modern heart surgery or about the advancements being made toward bloodless surgeries in general.

"That is — not true. — I know — Witnesses — who had heart surgery — with no blood," I say. He realizes he cannot deny that because he does not know. I wonder what he has learned in medical school. In spite of the praise I have heard of him, he scores a no-confidence vote in my estimation of him.

But I keep in mind what he says and keep my mind open to alternatives should I have to stay on Coumadin. After several times to the Protime Clinic with their portable prothrombin time monitor, I think I could operate one myself. If that were the case, I could still take long wilderness canoe trips to the Yukon if I was forced to continue Coumadin forever. I could be away a week or two or a month or more with one of these battery-operated monitors with the materials tucked into a dry box and still manage my dosages. I talk with the Protime Clinic nurse about it.

"— Can — anyone — buy — this machine?"

"Yes, some people use them in their homes."

"How — much?"

"This one costs about $1200. Calibrating it can be tricky, but you could do it."

In one of our brief conversations, I mention that to Dr. Reilly. He smiles and laughs, "You'd have to have a chemistry lab the size of a room to do that!"

I think back to the janitor's closet size lab here. He does not even know what is happening in his own Protime Clinic. Score one more no-confidence point.

"No, just a little box. — Just a finger poke. — Blood drop on paper — goes into box. — The nurse – does it."

Dr. Reilly looks incredulous though he tries to keep a straight face.

Little things like this put me on edge and wary of any recommendation Dr. Reilly makes. I am afraid that if his knowledge is unreliable in little things, he may be unknowing in big things, too. As a result, my feeble brain consumes an extraordinary amount of time evaluating the information he gives me.

The nurse in the Medical Group's first Protime Clinic is very good, and she keeps my therapeutic INR target of 2.5 within a tenth of a point for weeks. Then, the Medical Group moves into a bigger building and restructures the operation of the Protime Clinic. There is a new nurse, but I think she does a good job.

Unexpectedly, the nurse tells me she is not allowed to give me my dosages any more, that Dr. Reilly or his nurse will be contacting me. The system does not work as well as it had when it was in the "janitor's closet". My INR numbers are now always sub-therapeutic. More often than not, I am called by Dr. Reilly or his nurse with the information after hours. Clearly, they are too busy to deal with it and not as skilled as the protime nurse. Meanwhile, my INR range drops to 2.0 or less for months.

My appointment conversations with Dr. Reilly are too brief. He is no sooner into the room before he is off again. In one comment, he gives himself away. "We're supposed to spend only fifteen minutes per patient. That is eleven minutes with the patient and four minutes to dictate the report." He can do his talking part in that eleven minutes, but it does not leave much time for me to counter or ask questions. It takes me more than the usual amount of time to mull over a thought in my head, to think up some key words and to arrange them in different ways to construct a sentence that would make sense.

Our appointments are often agonizingly ineffectual. He is always in a hurry to be away. Even when I am not watching the clock, I can tell when the ten minute point has come. He has his hand on the door knob.

One minute for bye-bye and he has not gotten to my questions. Yes, twist, click and he is out the door. Any unfinished business is left for the next one which necessitates more appointments and wasted time. It would make more sense to stack up several appointments in a row so I would not waste so much time away from work and have the anxiety of unresolved questions lingering between appointments.

For that reason, I start requesting copies of my reports. Reading them takes a lot of time because I am such a slow reader. But it is good to be able to go over the material again at my leisure. Sometimes I have missed a point, and sometimes he has missed one of mine. If Frank has not been with me, I will not have notes at all. I also start writing questions and clarification to be delivered to Dr. Reilly before our next appointment.

If he has run out the door before I can say, "I need a mammogram," I write a note to him. Usually, I drop it off for his nurse to deliver it to him. Sometimes it works. Sometimes it does not. If I do not hear from the nurse or Dr. Reilly in a few days, I call and talk with the nurse. "— This — is — Carol Schultz. — I — need — a — m – ma-a-mam - o - grrr - graaa-a-am -mo -gram."

"A mammogram? Did Dr. Reilly say you needed one?"

While I am composing a response, I am also thinking without words: *Heck no, he is always too busy to notice things like that. He does not read any of the reports from my former doctors to discover that. And, he gives me no time to ask!!*

"No, — no Reilly. — Dr. Glenn's office. — Before my stroke. — When I got home. — They said. — They said when I got home — to get one."

Creating lists for the doctor takes its toll. The toll is a pervasive insomnia largely due from my empty brain spinning endlessly, looking for, hoping for the word it needs to say to the doctor the next day and the need to somehow remember the word until the next day so it can be used. Usually there is only searching, searching through a sleepless night.

The next day, it starts again. The difference is that now my eyes are open. I sit in front of the computer or a pad of paper during long periods of emptiness while I am looking for the right words to write. Looking, looking. Sometimes I can copy words from material I am *reading* as a basis for my writing. Still, it may take three hours to a day to write a paragraph and three days after that with corrections before it makes sense. Even at that, I find mistakes in my final draft.

Appointment by appointment, one concern at a time, Dr. Reilly attempts to address my ailments. The blood counts, chest x-rays and electrocardiogram procedures from my ER visit at the hospital show nothing alarming.

> **Dr. Reilly's report:**
> Normal stress echocardiogram with excellent wall motion improvement with exercise, and a low likelihood of coronary artery disease.
>
> Dyspnea (shortness of breath) is resolved. [I credit it to the stabilization of my INR numbers. He credits it to my being better conditioned.]
>
> She does complain of difficulty sleeping. I reviewed behavioral changes that she could make to allow better sleep. These include exercise three to four hours prior to sleep, out of bed if not asleep in 10-15 minutes, write problems on a pad of paper so that she does not perseverate while trying to sleep. I gave insomnia literature to her.

Insomnia is a huge issue. If I am not mistaken, sleep deprivation is akin to torture. Some of Dr. Reilly's recommendations are not conducive to my living situation or within my ability. He gives me a brochure to read when it is very difficult for me to read at all. He suggests I should have a notebook next to the bed so I can write down notes if thoughts keep me awake. That might be all right if I could write my thoughts.

Once before an appointment, I have been able to sleep a little better but still far from normally. Reilly's notes: "Insomnia, resolved." Any small improvement for me, in his mind, is the final solution for my problems and that door is closed. For me, the torture continues unresolved.

Hormones

I complain of being hot and sweaty all times of the day. I do not have the words for *hot flashes*, but he must get the idea. He intends to broach the subject in November, but due to his ten minute limit per patient, it is delayed until December. By then it is almost three months since he first saw me in September.

I am not sure what he is talking about. He does not ask about the hot flashes. He asks silly questions: "Do you keep warmer than usual or do you get cold more easily?" I must look puzzled. "Is your husband colder than you are? Are you warmer than he is?" I think he is asking about how we dress when we go outside. Somehow, however, he must come to the conclusion that I am having hot flashes. His eyes light up and he smartly and knowingly says, "I think you are premenopausal. I think you need estrogen!"

I know that. I am beyond premenopausal. I am in menopause. He could have asked me. I have not had a period for three months. My periods ended with my stroke when I stopped using birth control pills as a hormone replacement therapy. He thinks that if he prescribes estrogen it will be the cure all to end all, and his grin is because he would then be able to check off one of my problems. The problem with Dr. Reilly's quick fix is that both Dr. Braun and Dr. Glenn have told me not to use estrogen since it correlates with the formation of clots. Stroke.

I am taken aback and can only stare at Dr. Reilly for a minute while I compose a response. *What is the name of my doctor, the neurologist?* I have to think of Dr. Braun's name. The first name that comes to me is Rick. But no, I should not use that name. I need his last name. *Ahhh,* the spelling of his name finds its place in my head. *Ahhh — B-r-a-u-n.* Then a place in my mouth, "Braun, — Dr. Braun says, — no es-tro—es-tro-gen."

Dr. Reilly wants to disagree but he cannot. He does not want to counter another doctor in front of a patient. Reluctantly, his response is, "Well, Dr. Braun must have his reasons to say that." I can only wonder. It has been three months without a period since my stroke. I have counted them. That also means it has been three months since Dr. Reilly started working with me. In three months, he has not yet looked at my records from Dr. Braun and Dr. Glenn where they say "no estrogen".

Dr. Reilly dismisses me with a lab order. Later, I find it is for the same FSH test that Dr. Glenn gave showing my estrogen levels practically non-existent – three months before. Dr. Reilly misses a lot by not checking my history from other doctors. In the meantime I have waited months. Uncomfortably waiting in a state of tension not understanding what is happening to my health.

So, estrogen is what I need to eliminate my hot flashes? Yet I must not take estrogen. What is the solution? Is there an alternative to estrogen? I've spent my lifetime spurning any book or magazine that speaks to a woman's life style or a woman's health. Unfortunately, that has made me ill prepared for this stage of my life. Suddenly I am thrust into unfamiliar territory searching for remedies to these hormone problems. The logical way to learn in this age is to read. But I do not really read yet. Nevertheless, at a drug store while I am waiting for a prescription, my attention is drawn to the paperback books near the pharmacy. There are some health books. Herbs, vitamins, supplements, men's and women's subjects. I scan through some books to find something that might speak to me.

To call what I do as scanning is not really accurate. I cannot scan because I cannot really read. I am wading through the books. One word at a time. One strange new word at a time. Sound it out. Does it sound right? No. Try saying it a different way. With each word. At the end of the sentence, make a run at it again to see if I understand what the sentence says. At the end of the paragraph, make a run of the sentences. Does the paragraph make sense? Have I learned anything?

In the midst of this, a woman comes up. "Carol, how are you?"

I know this woman though her name does not come to mind. She is a customer. She and her family have come on the cross-country ski vacations we sponsor through the store. I am sure she knows I have had a stroke, but it is still embarrassing to be caught reading these books when I cannot actually read them. It must be obvious I do not know what I am doing.

"Hi. I don't have many words. I can't — take — es – estro — estrogen. I have hot — hot — you know."

"Hot flashes?"

"Yes, hot flashes. — Something else. — Looking for. — Looking for something else."

She says she has a collection of material about alternative therapies for women in menopause. She has even given classes about it before. She invites me to her home to look over the material. She will talk with me about it. *Wow! What a Godsend.*

What she shares with me and what I unearth myself is revealing. The first thing I realize is that when I discontinued the birth control pills suddenly, I was put into an exaggerated state of estrogen withdrawal.

It all fits. Many of the menopause symptoms fit the same ailments I thought were related to my starting Coumadin. It's been more than three months and no doctor warned me this might happen when they had me stop the pill abruptly. All the reasons that sent me back to the ER were due to estrogen withdrawal. What a waste! You would think that Glenn or Braun would have warned me about it, and it should not have taken Reilly three months to finally come around to the idea I had a hormone problem.

The challenge now is to find an alternative to estrogen to smooth out my symptoms. Of all the material I accumulate, the most interesting is a book called **What Your Doctor May Not Tell You About Menopause** by John R. Lee, M.D. with Virginia Hopkins. He speaks of a concept called "unopposed estrogen." He explains that unopposed estrogen is unopposed to progesterone. He also refers to it as "estrogen dominance". Some people discount his theories saying he bases them only on scientific reasoning, related medical research and limited clinical evidence without specific large double-blind studies. Others substantiate him. Dr. Lee makes some bold statements:

> ... in most menopausal women, estrogen levels are below that necessary for pregnancy but sufficient for other normal body functions...[1]

> I recommend you have a goal of getting off estrogen altogether ... Since postmenopausal women continue to make estrogen (primarily in their body fat). Many women find that estrogen supplementation can be eliminated altogether five to six months after starting the progesterone. The presence of progesterone makes estrogen receptors more sensitive, so that your own estrogen is sufficient.[2]

> Menopausal symptoms are caused not so much by declining hormone levels as by an *abrupt* drop in hormones.[3]

> Estrogen works especially well for hot flashes ...

> However, because progesterone is a biochemical precursor to estrogen, it alone is often sufficient to restore estrogen levels

---

1   *What Your Doctor May Not Tell You About Menopause* by John R. Lee, M.D., with Virginia Hopkins, pg. 48.
2   Ibid, pg. 276.
3   Ibid, pg. 314.

to normal and eliminate these symptoms.[4]

I pore over, with great difficulty, the material I am accumulating. I am particularly interested in knowing more about the advisability of using natural progesterone supplements. I take notes from the parts that seem most pertinent to share with Dr. Reilly. Since I am not skilled enough to communicate my questions verbally, I write down the material to present it to him. At an appointment a month later, he acknowledges he has seen the notes I gave him. He does not want anything to do with what he calls a "black box", which is his way of saying he knows nothing about natural progesterone.

Well, at least he admits he does not know anything about hormones. The problem is, he is not interested in knowing more either.

"Tell you what," he says. "I will find the best hormone doctor for you in Bellingham. My nurse will call you."

Now we are going somewhere! Dr. Reilly's nurse calls to say she has made an appointment for me with Dr. Mardee [not her name]. I know of her. She is a local GYN. I prepare my questions for her ahead of time so she can read them because I will not remember all the words I will need. She receives me enthusiastically, but she is not interested in considering natural progesterone therapy. She agrees with Glenn and Braun I should not be taking estrogen. She suggests my best course is to do nothing. Eventually the hot flashes will go away. She says, of course, that might take six years or longer. She says her patients try taking various herbs and supplements to decrease their hot flashes, but they are of questionable effectiveness. She says she could prescribe Clonidine for me. Sometimes it helps.

"What is that?"

She says, "It is a blood pressure drug."

I say, "I — already — take — b-blood pressure — drug."

"You'd take two."

It did not seem reasonable to me to double up on my blood pressure drug, and she did not offer an explanation.

---

4   Ibid, pg. 321.
     (Permission granted by Grand Central Publishing, Hachette Book Group, Inc.)

I leave her office with an empty feeling. The door mat said, "Welcome", and a hand written note by the open door said, "We are expecting you." But no one was home. Dr. Mardee was not home for me. *What a waste.* I resolve to keep looking further.

On the way back to work, I stop at a naturopathic office. The naturopathic doctor here was recommended to me as one who works with women's hormones. I do not have her name with me but I know this is her office. I look for her name on the front of the building and on her certificates in the front office so I can request her name. There is a lot of rustling and talk in the back room. The receptionist comes out followed by a very thin, tense woman who is moving very quickly and nervously. I sense she is under a lot of pressure. The receptionist asks what I want.

Looking at one of the framed certificates, I say, "I — wonder — if — Doctor Larson (not the true name) — is in."

The receptionist refers me to the nervous woman behind her. "This is Dr. Larson."

Dr. Larson says, "What do you want?"

Since the doctor is apparently under pressure and short on time, I feel I need to explain why it will take longer than usual for me to speak. "I had a stroke. — It took my words. — I don't have many words. — I cannot take estrogen — but — I have — hot — flashes. — Could you help — about — natural pro - gest - er - one?"

"Hormones can be tricky," she says. While her receptionist is looking at the appointment calendar, Dr. Larson interrupts, telling her, and by that to me, "I am really too busy getting things ready for this project right now. I won't be seeing new patients for at least six weeks." I thank them while thinking I really do not want to wait six weeks.

Apparently, the medical establishment in Bellingham does not want anything to do with natural alternatives to pharmaceutical hormone drugs. I am going to have to find a naturopathic doctor somewhere who has a handle on these issues. I do not know where to start. However, by chance, Frank and I have dinner with the Parkers a couple days later. Manfred is a dedicated follower of every natural alternative imaginable. Diane has recently had occasion to seek out a solution to her own hormonal balancing problems. At a large naturopathic clinic in the Seattle area, she has found a naturopath who prescribed and monitored progesterone levels for her. That sounded like a doctor I need, a doctor who can look at all my health history and tell me if progesterone is an option for me. And if not, what other alternatives might be compared to estrogen.

It takes a few more weeks learning a few more words to have enough courage to call for an appointment with the clinic. Courage, because making the phone call with my limited vocabulary and an impaired understanding of the spoken word will be difficult.

Soon after I start using progesterone under this naturopathic doctor's supervision, I start to have a much better sense of well being. For the first time since my stroke, I can sleep soundly most nights. An aching joint pain diminishes. Blood pressure stabilizes to the point I can discontinue the blood pressure medicine. Fatigue decreases to the point I can increase exercise, get through the day and start attending some evening meetings. Hot flashes become faint memories compared to those of the past. With the return of better health, I find I am better able to cope with the prospect of having heart surgery to close my PFO (patent foramen ovale).

PFO closure – pros and cons

Our doctor friend, Dr. John Arnold, and my neurologist, Dr. Braun, are supplying us with medical studies and articles on the pros and cons of closing my PFO. All of the material is written for doctors so the language is demanding to the layman. Frank reads it fairly easily; I must spend hours wading through each paragraph with a medical dictionary in hand. What we find out about PFOs is alarming.

> The PFO is a natural inter-atrial channel allowing a functional right-to-left shunt of placental oxygenated blood and closing during birth by a higher pressure in the left atrium. It is possible that the FO is not closed in one third of persons below 29 years old and in about one fourth of those above 30 years old in an autopsy of 965 normal hearts…. It is known that PFO is a risk factor for thrombo-embolic events in all age groups.

> … contrast echocardiography has clearly demonstrated that microbubbles can cross through the PFO even if there is not elevated pulmonary-artery pressure…. Indeed, it may be possible

to induce a reversal inter-atrial gradient, either spontaneously or during a cough test or a Valsalva maneuver. The phenomenon may explain why in some cases, cerebral embolism of paradoxical origin may be triggered by straining efforts, such as in sport or in defecation.[5]

It is distressing to learn that 25% of the population has an open PFO. *Shoot, that's a lot of people running around with a PFO. It is not uncommon. It's a miracle we don't have people falling onto the sidewalk from stroke all the time.* One article claims that stroke from the presence of a PFO is rare. However, risk of stroke correlates with the size of the PFO. Transesophageal echocardiograms (TEE) do not see well enough to actually measure the size of the PFO. But since mine is *fairly significant*, my risk is fairly significant. It is a wonder I have not had a stroke sooner. I have been at risk since birth.

I also wonder why a doctor would prescribe an HRT drug or birth control pills – known stroke risks – without eliminating the presence of a significant PFO. Granted, the procedure is expensive, but those in the medical profession must know the medical costs of stroke. There is not only the medical expense but the loss of earnings to the victims and their families. I think if it were all added up, the cost of a TEE and the closure of a PFO would be a fraction of the cost of treating a stroke patient. (According to the American Heart Association, the estimated direct and indirect cost of stroke in 2008 was $65.5 billion.)

There is more talk about the benefit of closing an open PFO as opposed to ignoring it. There are four therapeutic options to treat an open PFO. One is the use of what they call antiaggregants. Basically, aspirin type drugs. The second is anticoagulants or warfarin type drugs. The third is a transcatheter closure of the PFO with a mechanical device. The forth is surgical closure of the PFO by means of open heart surgery using sutures.

The antiaggregants (aspirin) therapy is also called antiplatelet therapy. In this therapy, drugs bind irreversibly to platelets to prevent blood clotting.

---

5   The interest of surgical closure of patent foramen ovale after stroke: a preliminary open study of 8 cases; *Neurological Research*, 1998, Volume 20 June; ©1998 Forefront Publishing Group 0161—6412/98/040297-05, permission by Maney Publishing, www.maney.co.uk/journals/ner and www.ingentaconnect.com/content/maney/nres

Anticoagulants therapy acts to control the thickness of the blood by using Coumadin as I do now. I already do not like the constant testing required while using Coumadin, and there is always the risk/benefit ratio in using it. For example, if one's INR threshold is high or not controlled adequately, the risk of major bleeding can be as high as 11% per year.

Frank and I spend a lot of time going through various articles about the transcatheter closures. There are button types and umbrella types. Most work, but some get lost and need to be retrieved. A few leak. In general, the studies consider them successful and their use may decrease the recurrence of stroke while letting the patient be free of risk from anticoagulants. While the articles are fairly recent (within the last two years), the devices' effectiveness and complication rate are not yet established.

The last therapeutic option is open heart surgery to close the PFO. Evidently, it is quite effective. Stroke recurrence is rare even without anticoagulant therapy after the surgery. The drawback is that it is major surgery.

In weighing the pros and cons, I come away believing the best option will be the open heart surgery closure. The transcatheter closure procedure is tempting because it is faster without the potential complications from surgery. However, I have a hard time imagining a hard metal object in my heart pinched between two fleshy heart chambers. I imagine its edges rubbing against my pulsing heart beat with every stroke. Grating, digging into it, causing a constant source of scar tissue. At least that is what I imagine. Also, the information currently available suggests uncertainties regarding the devices.

About the same time I have been deciphering the PFO closure material, Dr. Reilly says to me, "I've been talking to a hematologist here about your stroke and DVT (deep vein thrombosis). He said I should do a more detailed phospholipids antibody panel on you to see if you have a propensity to clotting."

Propensity to clotting? No one has mentioned that possibility at all, yet there is such a thing? What the heck! Dr. Reilly tells me it is a disorder I have lived with all my life. If my tendency to clot could be determined with a blood test, why did the nurse practitioner not run that test first before she prescribed birth control pills? The pill only compounded my risk to stroke?

We seek second opinions about the phospholipids antibody panel tests. The rounds of the doctors would be comical if the subject was not so serious. Here we are trying to make informed and educated decisions, and the doctors do not agree.

Dr. Arnold took a look at my lab reports from the hospital and said, "You already did that and the results were all low negative."

Dr. Braun says, "Your tests at the hospital were all low."

But evidently, the new antiphospholipids test has more parts than the hospital test did. When the test comes back, Dr. Reilly is practically gloating. The test shows that two parts of a multiple level screen are slightly positive. This is the confirmation Dr. Reilly has been looking for as the definitive confirmation of his insisting I stay on Coumadin the rest of my life. There would be no reason to close the PFO since it would only eliminate clots coming from the lower extremities. In the presence of a hyperphospholipid syndrome condition, I would still be at risk of stroke from clots anywhere in my body.

Frank:
Then in January 1999, one blood test showed that Carol had a blood disorder called hyperphospholipid syndrome, which greatly increased the chance of a clot anywhere in the body. We were walking a tightrope with the Coumadin: too little, and she could have a stroke from a clot; too much, and she stood a chance of a hemorrhage in the brain or serious bleeding from a slight cut.

I schedule an appointment with the hematologist. He is very thorough, sincere, and caring. His advice to us is that I should stay chronically on Coumadin. In view of the antiphospholipids results, he says, closing the PFO is a moot point.

However, when I get his report and Dr. Reilly's, they both suggest I will be better off doing both. In other words, I should stay on Coumadin *and* close the PFO. This is in conflict with what they had said to me when I was with them in their offices so it makes me feel distrustful of them both. What if I had never read their reports? How would I have known I might be better off by *also* closing the PFO?

Dr. Braun reviews the positive presence of hyperphospholipid syndrome with me. He is not sure I have it. He says the syndrome is characterized by recurrent spontaneous abortions, lupus, autoimmune diseases and thromboses. While I did have a DVT (deep vein thrombosis), he feels the canoe trip, the long car ride and the fact I was on birth control pills contributed to my stroke. That was one time and otherwise, I have no characteristics of the syndrome. I also notice a note in the lab report suggests there may be a 5% error in the results: "However, up to 5% of serum specimens from healthy controls may exhibit values in the moderate positive range." Maybe I am in the 5%.

Not long after, Dr. Braun calls me at work to say he has been getting second opinions for me. He has discussed my case with a rheumatologist in Bellingham and then with a doctor at Virginia Mason Hospital. Dr. Braun says their advice is to run my antiphospholipid screen again at six months. If these resolve, then he recommends me staying off estrogen, take aspirin, and close the PFO.

> **Frank:**
> What was the risk involved in the surgery? With the phospholipids profile, would the operation do any good if she could have a clot form anywhere at any time? We made the rounds of doctors' offices, got lots of advice, and finally settled down with the idea that the phospholipids could be a temporary situation, and if the high levels resolved themselves, she would have the PFO closed surgically.

At long last in July of 1999, we get a call from Dr. Braun's office. His nurse reports: "Lab results of 6/9 great per Dr. Braun. He will discuss results with her more fully…" At my next appointment with him, he shows me the phospholipids have completely resolved. He recommends I close the PFO and then go on aspirin.

As a fixer by nature, I am ready now to fix my PFO. Frank is not as sure, but supports my decision.

> **Frank:**
> I was really concerned now. As long as she couldn't have the surgery, I didn't have to worry about it. Now, it was looming up in the near future and I dreaded the thought of Carol having her sternum split, the surgical risk, and the pain and recovery

period that she would have to endure. But it was her life, and it had to be her decision entirely. In this one, I was just along for the ride, like it or not.

Carol started increasing her physical workload every week, training for the operation as if it were a marathon ski race approaching. She worked out on Chuckanut Mountain with her ski poles, hiked, used a rubber band exerciser for upper body strength, added vitamin supplements to her diet, and got as ready as anyone ever did for the challenge of the open heart surgery. We shopped around for a heart surgeon, but had no difficulty in choosing Dr. Jim Douglas. The logistics were a lot easier to handle if it were done locally, and his reputation among local physicians and surgeons was excellent.

At long last, in September, after an appointment with the local heart surgeon, Dr. Jim Douglas, I set the date for my open heart surgery PFO closure for October 20, 1999.

Part Five

Quest for Words

The Void?

Concurrent with the challenges of running the medical gauntlet, I am also trying to learn to speak – and to better understand what is going on in my brain.

So, the void? What is in there?

Frank later tells me, "Carol, you had words in your head."

"No," I tell him. "Having thoughts in your head is different from having words for them."

One thinks a lot when one is deprived of words. How it is that one can even wonder and have thoughts without words? Sitting on the canoe chair out on the deck, I watch. It is amazing how much there is to look at when one cannot read.

There is a stand of second growth fir trees across the creek. Seeing them makes me wonder about their eventuality and mine. Eventually, each tree will fall to the ground. Fancifully, I wonder. *When one of those great old growth fir trees falls crashing to the ground, has the crash made a sound if no one has heard?* Then my mind wanders to a more personal parallel. *When one no longer understands the spoken word and can no longer speak, does one no longer have thoughts in their head?*

It is unfortunate in our society that intelligence is too often equated to one's speech dexterity. Because I speak so poorly, some assume I do not have thoughts in my head. Therefore, they think I do not have intelligence. I know I have thoughts, but without words to express them, my intelligence is suspect. How true is that of those with more severe aphasic strokes? Grandfather Schultz never learned to speak after his stroke.

)id he still have thoughts? It is embarrassing now to think I had assumed he had also lost his intelligence, and maybe he had not.

The persistent challenge for me is to be able to cross this aphasic void with words. How? If the stroke has actually destroyed the language centers in my brain and if that is permanent, how can there be learning? Recovery? There is nothing to work with. Nothing. And it feels that way, too. Nothing. There is nothing in the void to hang on to. Nothing that would reasonably suggest there might be a bridge to span the void.

Nothing. I have worked with nothing before. Doing with nothing in the past usually meant doing with less and creating something by using whatever materials were available. My parents had shown the way. When Mom wanted a bookshelf with drawers in the kitchen, Dad built one. When she needed a rug for the living room and there was no money to buy one, she braided one using scraps. When Dad's easy chair fell apart except for the cushions, he salvaged discarded walnut boards from a firewood pile and framed a chair of boards to hold the cushions.

When it was time for Frank and me to think about having a house with no financial means, we looked at our resources. Frank had been a logger. I had been raised in the woods. We were both accustomed to hard labor and building a log home seemed not out of reason. We purchased trees from the Forest Service and went to work.

Later, when it was time for our boys to have desks, and we did not have enough money to buy them or even to purchase plywood to construct them, I contemplated. What did we have? What were my resources? It was apparent we had tools and raw materials. We still had a stockpile of lumber. Rough-sawn 2x6 fir planks we had milled from the long butts of our house logs. A pile of left-over cedar seconds from the gable end siding. So, I designed the desks to fit the materials available. Ripped and planed, sawed, routed, glued and screwed. It was more time consuming and more complicated than buying store-bought, but it sufficed. Somehow, it always seemed that in spite of having nothing, there were always resources to draw from.

My predicament is more difficult than that now, and finds parallel in this story:

> A scientist chatting with God said to him, "How do you feel about yourself now that man is able to create life?"

"Oh, really?" said God. "How do to you go about creating life?"

"Easy," the scientist said. "The first thing we do is start with a little dirt ..."

"Stop, stop right there," said God. "Get your own dirt!"

Well, that is what I need! I need my own dirt. My own resources. I have worked with nothing before but this is different. There is not only *nothing* in my language center; there are no resources either. No dirt to draw on. Is the aphasic stroke victim helpless to help herself? Desperately, I count on the speech profession to show me the way.

Looking for my own dirt

It has been almost two weeks since my stroke and four speech sessions later. I am in Ms. Sands' office again looking forward to learning the words she used with me from the coloring book page. But, no, that page does not appear. Today is a new piece of paper. This one is full of words. Just words, not in sentences. They are in big print scattered all over the page. There are some short ones and some long ones. They start with any old letter. They do not seem to have a pattern of letters among them. She asks me to say the words.

Just out of nowhere she asks me to say the words? I am bewildered by the words and her request. I stare at them as if Ms. Sands thinks that if I stare at them long enough I will *remember* the words. Am I supposed to learn them by osmosis?

She says, "Go ahead. Sound them out."

What does that mean? With no reference to the sounds that the letters make on the page, I try each word with many sound attempts. Each word comes with many ways of trying to make a sound. Sometimes after many attempts, one will sound like it had been in my memory before. She helps me with some words, but I do not finish the page. Ms. Sands lets me take this page home to learn. Is this how I learn to read and say words? Ms. Sands certainly did not give me any other ideas. So is this the way to learn? To just start making stabs at the letters until a word seems to sound familiar?

It does not seem right to learn words this way. She expects me to be able to say the words, yet she gives me no idea of how to do that. This is not the way I learned to read when I was young. How was I taught in school?

Nevertheless, I go home and practice the page with Frank's help, but neither of us understands how this exercise is of value. The words on that page do not make sense. They are just random words. None of them relate to the other, and I do not know that I will be able to use them. Maybe it is just an exercise to practice moving my mouth around. Yet, I persist with each new word going through the same ritual of experimenting with many sounds until one feels familiar.

I continue to work with the speech therapist though I am never sure why. There seems to be no rhyme or reason to her teaching. Each time I come, she arbitrarily runs her finger down the many speech therapy aids from her shelves and at random stops and pulls out a work book, randomly picks out a page or two and copies it for my lesson. There are pages on digraphs and diphthongs, antonyms and synonyms, alphabetization, filling missing words, and definitions I cannot read. Words about words I do not understand and did not even know existed before my stroke. Each homework piece comes with words I am supposed to be able to read and to say. I need to be able to read to complete the assignment, but she does not teach me to read. That is left up to me. I spend exhausting hours with each two page assignment. My completed work, though, does not begin to show the extraordinary time I have spent forming the neat words penciled on each line.

In order to complete Ms. Sands' assignments, I need more words than she gives me. In an attempt to learn more words, I read baby books at home supplied by our friend, Julie Fleetwood. Frank and I took them to Ms. Sands thinking she would be pleased. But her response was, "We don't use these. They are demeaning to adults!" The implication is, of course, that they are beneath me, too, and I shouldn't use them.

I had to wonder more about Ms. Sands. How could these books be demeaning to an adult when the adult's reading level was that of a three year old? Is it not logical to start teaching at the beginning? When we teach cross-country skiing, we do not start beginners at the top of the steepest hill and expect them to swoop down the hill expertly the first time just because they are adults! No, we start at the bottom and teach in gentle, progressive stages. To me, starting with preschool readers is logical. I think they do not teach speech therapists to teach what I need.

Ms. Sands always starts a session with conversation. At first I think she is interested in me personally, but I soon suspect she just wants me to practice saying words. She always asks what I have done since the last session. Of course, I have difficulty remembering the many things I have done, so I start a list on yellow lined paper to record my achievements and show her the list at the beginning of each session. If I have tried to read an article from the newspaper, I write down *paper*. If I have been reading a kid's book, I write down *book* with the title I have copied from the book cover.

Ms. Sands says, "You are reading more than I thought you were."

Heck, yes. How am I going to learn to read the material you send home with me if I don't learn to read? You're not teaching me! Somehow I have to do it myself, and this is the only way I know! Neither does Ms. Sands seem to know I must read aloud. The letters of the word on the page mean nothing to me until I hear the word with its printing for it to say something to me. In the process of sounding out the words I am reading, and I am also learning to talk.

One day her comment is, "Why are you reading so much? There are other things wrong with you!" The implication, of course, is that I am wasting my time reading. But, intuitively, I feel it is imperative to learn to read aloud to be able to talk. Why can she not understand that?

I manage to tell Ms. Sands I am not able to understand phone numbers when people give them to me over the phone. To her credit, she helps. At first she calls out numbers to me as I write them down. Then she checks them against her answer list. After a few cycles of that, she thinks I am doing well enough, though I still make a lot of mistakes.

I know she is bored but I want more. I say, "More."

She produces audio tapes for me. When I get home, I listen to the tape and write down the numbers I hear. The only way I have of checking my answers is to listen to the tape again, but that does not work very well. I made mistakes in the first place because I did not comprehend the number the first time.

At the next session, Ms. Sands checks my answers against her answer sheet. Seeing that, I want a copy of the answers, too. I can check my work myself and have instant feed-back. I can analyze my work to see if there is a pattern to my mistakes. I can learn more quickly. The way things are, I have to wait until the next session to see how well or poorly I have done. A lot of time is lost waiting.

I say to Ms. Sands, "I— want."

"You want a copy of the answers?"

"Yes, — to — see — if — right."

Obviously reluctant to hand over a copy of the answer sheet to me, she says, "You might cheat."

She is kidding, of course. But no, she is serious. That is an insult to my integrity, and for a moment I am crushed. In seconds, however, embarrassment turns to a controlled anger. *Who does she think I am? Who is she? Does she want me to learn or not?*

"No, — no cheat. — Give me!" I say to Ms. Sands. *Cheat who? What difference is it who grades my homework? Who is she to limit my learning by not trusting me to check my own work?*

Ms. Sands is a different breed. One time, I show up on a day the receptionist has double scheduled her. Coming into the center after an appointment elsewhere, she sees me waiting in the lobby. Consulting her schedule with the receptionist, she says, "I didn't realize you were coming. I can fit you in for a short session if you want. I will find something for you to do." That was fine for me. Then at the end of the session, she apologizes she does not have anything ready for me to work on at home.

"That is okay," I say, "I — will work — myself." A simple statement not out of the ordinary, I think.

But Ms. Sands says something I will never forget. She says, "Work on something yourself? What can you do for yourself?" I have wondered, too, whether I would be able to do anything myself, but to hear it from her now is an affront. It dawns on me that in spite of all the work I have been doing on my own, and as hard I have tried to show her how much work I have been doing myself, it has not registered with her.

Another time, I try to explain to Ms. Sands that I need to say the word again and again. Need to hear it again and again. Practice.

She responds with a questioning silence. Then says, "Practice?"

"Yes, pr – prac — tice."

She is not following. Her face searches me like she has never heard the word. "What do you mean?"

Is this a strange idea to her? "You know. — Like — mu - sic. — Music. — Have — you — pl - played — an — in - stru - ment?"

She has. "Yes."

"Then — like — that. — You pr - prac - tice. — You practice — sc - scales. — You practice — music. — Over — and — over. — Again — and — again till you — know it. — You can – play – it – with-out — thinking. — Same – with – words."

You practice the scale or the piece again and again until it finds a place in your brain until it becomes automatic – without thinking. That's why I need to practice words.

"Oh!" she says as if the lights had turned on.

Oh, oh, come on Ms. Sands, I think, *how commonsensible can it be?*

—⁓—

As a youngster, I once asked my father why one of the volunteers, who frequented the Boy Scout Camp Bradford where we lived, always seemed to make a mess of everything he did. If he was painting, he spilled the paint. When placing a ladder to climb on, it would slide off and he would fall with it. If he was chopping wood he never thought about keeping the axe away of his legs, and he would get cut. "Why isn't he smart?" I asked.

Dad thought and very carefully answered. "Well, Jack means good. He's got lots of intelligence. He's an important lawyer." Then, he added deliberately in his Hoosier jargon, "He's got lots of smarts, but he ain't got no common sense."

—⁓—

Ms. Sands must have lots of smarts. After all she has lots of initials behind her name on her business card. It must be the common sense part that is missing.

Ms. Sands has me write letters. She knows I want to go back to work, so she sets a goal for me to be able to write business letters. The problem is that even if I can think of the word I need, I cannot get the letters for the word written down well enough for the spell checker to find it. Finally, when I learn to say the word *spell*, I complain to Ms. Sands that I cannot spell.

She says, "Well, I don't know much about spelling," and casually pulls out a piece of paper titled, *Spelling Helps*. "Here, maybe this will help you," she says and hands it to me as if this is going to solve all my spelling problems.

Heck, I can read only with great difficulty, and these rules are too complicated for me to comprehend. Is this the best you can do? I cannot see why spelling does not go hand-in-hand with speech. To me, it ought to.

Nevertheless, I give it a try. Soon, though, it is evident there must be missing steps in the progression of being able to spell, and I am wasting my time not having them. At one of our sessions, Ms. Sands selects again from the list of business letter topics saying, "For the next time, I want you to write a business letter in response to the third situation listed here."

I stare at her a moment. I think about how fruitless this exercise is until I can spell. It is a waste of my time always starting at the top where she always seems to think I should be. My response to her is, "NO! — No, — I — can — not — spell!" I have decided I will not write any more letters for her!

About the same time I am having trouble spelling with Ms. Sands I get a call from Julie Fleetwood. She was Tom and Tim's kindergarten teacher and is a wonderful person for me to listen to over the phone. She speaks very distinctly and deliberately with a measured slowness. I can understand her. She has been away for a few weeks and wonders how I am doing. I explain as best I can over the phone with limited stammering words that I am practicing the books she has loaned me. I have more words, but I do not know how to write them down. I tell her I do not *hear* them.

"Oh," she says, "I can teach you to spell. When can you come over to my house?"

Ms. Sands works with me a little longer, but soon declares she has helped me as much as she can. "Besides," she says, "now you have a spelling teacher." The next session with Ms. Sands will be the last one with her and she will test me to see how much progress I have made. I have had 25 speech therapy lessons over the past three months. The last will be the 26th, which, incidentally, is the annual limit of my health insurance therapy coverage. No insurance, no therapy.

In the last session, Ms. Sands pulls out the same coloring book page she used with me in the beginning. The one with the house and the garage, the man and the boy, the ladder, grass and bushes. "What do you see?" she asks. I do better this time than I did the first time, but I cannot help but think this is "dirty pool". In the full three months she has worked with me, she never once taught me the words I need to describe the illustration. If I have learned any of them, I have learned them incidentally.

Ms. Sands is complimentary about the progress I have made and thinks I will be able to go back to work. I do not think she knows how much I do not know. I still do not know if I graduated or if I had been fired.

—〰—

It is true that time has passed, and speech therapy methods have changed since my experience with Ms. Sands. But at the time, I found speech therapy extremely frustrating. I kept going back thinking something would materialize for me, but more often than not, I left each session with an unfulfilled feeling. I did not want to learn words by rote. I did not want to spend the next seven years of my life learning to speak, to read and write again as if I were progressing from three to ten years old. I wanted to start at the bottom, but I wanted results quickly. I wanted tools, methods, progression, organization and planning. Those concepts were lacking. I had no vocabulary to express my dissatisfaction, yet somewhere in my head was a notion there was a teaching concept that had worked for me as a child. It was probably called phonics, but as I did not have the word for it, I was unable to ask for it. Although I am sure my speech therapy met the standard of care, I am sure had it been my only experience with speech therapy, I would still not be able to speak, or read, or write effectively.

Fortunately, the discontent I felt from my speech therapy has mellowed with time. I now know more of the complexities of the task, and the difficulties the therapist faces. Types and degrees of aphasia are so varied that each patient requires a unique recovery program from a gifted, creative therapist.

Especially in aphasia, the therapist's job is not an easy one, and the value of effective speech therapy cannot be underestimated. If the first therapy series is ineffective, the patient may not only be left untreated – but may also feel abandoned. Good therapists deserve wholehearted praise for their often unappreciated work.

—〜—

Any which way I can

Gratefully, Ms. Sands is not my only mentor. Since Ms. Sands is not filling in the slots enabling me to complete my assignments I depend largely on my family, my friends and my own initiative. Developing learning methods by myself is more a thrashing around than one of deliberately thinking. However, it is better than nothing.

> **Frank:**
> The first breakthrough was with Julie Fleetwood. She had a treasure trove of kindergarten reading books, which were just what Carol needed to learn to read at a basic level.

The first books Julie sends are made with thick cardboard pages so a toddler cannot tear them up. Each book teaches about one category of words. Each page has an illustration and one word at the bottom. The books are *I Can Count*; *I Can Read*; *I Know About Numbers*; *I Can*; *1, 2, 3*; and *Red, Blue, Yellow Shoe*. Then there is one book in regular paper, *Go, Dog, Go!*.

These are the ticket! These are common words I can use. I need to know my tummy and my nose and my colors and my numbers. I read the books aloud to practice saying the words.

> **Frank:**
> The simple books like *Go, Dog, Go!* and those by Dr. Seuss would keep us occupied for hours. We would sit on our deck in the morning sunlight and read the Sunday comics. Each week saw some improvement in Carol's reading. Another friend who helped a lot was Sue Juntunen who taught special education in Sedro-Woolley. She had a lot of insightful tricks to get the idea of connecting the words with what Carol was reading, which complemented Julie's teaching methods.

As good as they are, these books are not self-starters. I need help with the words. I need someone to say them to me first. Then I try to remember them and how to say them. Frank goes over them with me. Sometimes a friend comes by to read to me from a children's book. One of our former employees, Jodi Broughton, points to the words as she reads to me, and then she asks questions about the story. Of course, I have been too busy watching the words as she speaks so I miss the story. We have to start over again.

Dad always said, "In this family we never stand on ceremony." My logger husband tells me that *stand on ceremony* comes from Shakespeare. I did not know that, but from the way Dad would say it, I knew it meant getting a job done anyway we could – with minimal instruction – and quickly. We became proud in taking initiative to get a job done even when those higher up were not coming forth with suggestions, funds or support.

It is quickly apparent that if I am to recover from this stroke, I cannot stand on ceremony. There are not enough people in the whole world to be spoon-feeding me all the time. So, I find myself trying to read unassisted. *What is that word they said before*, I puzzle. *There is a bear patting its stomach. What is that word at the bottom of the page? What is that called?* "T-u-m-m-y". *Tummy.* "Tummy." That one came fairly quickly. The ones like *yellow* and *purple* are very difficult.

Unknowingly in the beginning, I try to use the names of the letters of the alphabet as a key to know how to say a word. Thus, *yellow* sounds out, "Wi-e-el-o-dub-el-u." For *purple*, I try to say "pe-u-ar-pe-el-e". It does not resemble anything I can remember ever hearing before. With that, I simply start stabbing at words with any sound I can imagine. Seemingly, it takes fourteen tries per word before the sounds find an echoing familiarity.

More than once, I practice my words aloud while Frank and Tim are present. Frank might be reading a magazine, Tim with a book across the table from me. I know I am a nuisance to them, but I am determined to learn words. It should have been embarrassing to me, but I am beyond embarrassment. I like to think they are engrossed in their reading and not paying attention to me. Then, Tim corrects a word I said. I look at him across the table where he has been reading a different book. I cannot see how he knows I had not said a word right. "Tim, — are you — watching?"

"No, Mom, you're not making sense."

Not exactly a bingo, but I am getting the idea I am not saying the right sounds with the words. Not only that, neither do I recognize the word coming out of my mouth. I am not hearing the word I have said myself.

Thus, comes my learning in fits and starts. Grab a bit of information from here and a bit from there. Accumulate the pieces hoping they will eventually make a whole. In one of those periods of helplessness when I am home alone, I practice the alphabet. I think I can say it. I can rattle it off, but do I really know it? I do not even know what words I say. Do I know what letter I say? On a page, I write the letters down in a column. Then I fold that under and write it down in the second column. Then I check them. If they do not match, I have left out a letter. So, again, one column after the other. If I am interrupted, I do not know what letter is next. I have to start again saying the letters aloud. I do not know what I am doing or why. It just seems that if I am to be able to read, to be able to talk, I ought to know the letters.

There is a limit to how much time I can spend *reading*. It is exhausting work. I am good for an hour or so until my throat is sore and my brain rebels. To rest, I have lunch on the deck sitting on the canoe chair with my lunch on the floor beside me – and watch. I can remember Tom as a preschooler leaning against the porch under the eave while it was raining outside. Watching. Just watching. Maybe singing a preschool song. And watching and listening. Content and dreaming as the rain came down around him.

I feel like a preschooler now like Tom was. I watch and dream like Tom did. I had wondered what his watching did for him. But as he grew up, I knew it had piqued his interest in many things about the out-of-doors, and he eventually acquired a large vocabulary that enabled him to describe the things around him. A vocabulary is what I need. So I watch. Maybe it will help.

Strangely enough on this late August day, a pair of large blue birds is building a nest. They are working in a fir bough that is hanging near the ground. One bird fusses placing a twig, poking it in here and there. The other bird is flitting around on the slope across the creek. He picks up a twig. Holds it in his beak. Appraises it carefully tilting it from side to side as if it will help him see it better. That looks like a good one to me, but no, he does not like it and drops it. He flits to another in a tree, or then to a bush, or onto the ground on the bank. He looks several times to find the perfect twig and flies back to the nest.

In the meantime, the other bird has been very carefully placing her one twig. Does he give his twig to her to let her place the twig in her nest? *Hmmmm. No.* They trade places. He perches on the limb and fusses over the placement of his twig while she goes to the creek bank to fret about finding her own perfect twig. When she returns, she places her twig, and he flies off to the creek to find one for himself.

That is peculiar. Not only is it August and they are nesting, but more interestingly, they are also very cooperative in their marriage. When Frank and I were building our home, I am not sure I was as cooperative and complacent about how things were built as this mommy bird is. If I never learn words from this experience, I will have learned from their example.

Had this stroke not taken my words, I would never have taken time to watch these birds nesting. I should have stood beside Tom and watched with him. So, what in the heck are these birds? I know them. I have known their names. They are birds, at least I have finally mastered that word. They are also blue. I learned the color from the toddlers' reader on colors. Logically, they could be called Bluebirds, but I know they are not Bluebirds. We had Bluebirds in Indiana but they were different. These are much bigger and they have pointed feathers on their head.

Why not look in the book with birds in it? I can leaf through the book and try my luck. There it is. They are Steller's Jays. *Jay*, I can remember fairly easily, but *Steller's* is much more difficult. It goes in too many places in my mouth to make it very easy to say. Can I shorten it to Blue Jay? Blue Jay? No, we had Blue Jays in Indiana, too. They were different. To say it correctly, I have to be able to say Steller's Jay. "S-t-el-ler's Jay. S-t-el-ler's Jay. S-t-el-ler's Jay". There is no peace in watching for me. Some count birds. I count words.

Another rest from reading aloud is to walk the interurban trail. But even there, I feel compelled to learn words. If Frank is with me, I ask for words. Names of trees. Names of flowers. Names of birds. "hh-Wat's that?" pointing to a bird.

Playfully he says, "That what?"

"That!" I respond.

"That bush?" he says.

"NO, THAT!" pointing at the bird again.

"That tree?" he says.

"NO! That bird!"

"Oh, the Robin?"

"NO! Cawww, cawww! B l Ue, no, B l Ack! That one."

"Oh," he says, "the crow?"

"Yes, again."

And he repeats *crow* for me until I can say it.

Another pastime when I am by myself is to count. Count numbers. Realizing I do not recognize numbers when they are spoken to me, I mistakenly think if I say my numbers often enough, they will all register. So I count steps by rote. "One, two, three, four, five, six, seven, eight, nine, ten,"… until I get to one hundred, if I get to a hundred. And I start over again, and again.

That works well enough until I start thinking about what number I am saying. "Seventy-seven. Seventy-seven? Seventy-seven?" *Where in the heck am I? What number is that?* I do not know it or what came before it or after it. *Where am I?*

Nothing to do but to start over again. Until – "Nineteen. Nineteen?" *What kind of number is that? Shoot, nothing to do but start over again.*

Then there are the numbers on the power poles along the trail. With deep concentration I think I am able to say the names of the numbers. "Nine – five – four – eight – six – seven – one." But I am not sure. As hard as I try to listen to the names of the numbers I say, I cannot be sure I say them correctly. But I try. Again. At each power post.

My good friend, Irene Rinn, is often at my side. She is constantly contributing to my learning words. In the first month I am advised not to drive and Irene visits often.

Irene:
We sit on the deck; you talk haltingly and with great effort, many times not able to say what you want to say. All our

sentences are stilted and dead-end alarmingly fast. There is no length or depth to it, and I find there is nowhere I can think of to go with this.

One day, you let me know that you want to go for pizza. When we look at the menu, you point at one spot and say you can't say that – and I see that you are pointing at the word *mushrooms* in the toppings list. I am struck again by how this can be – that you can remember the thing you want, remember where it is located on the menu, but cannot say the word. This confounds me, and I wonder again what this is like on the inside.

I want salad, too. The waitress asks, "Whatkindofdressing?"

Whoops. This is the typical waitress mantra thing. I know she is asking which salad dressing I want, but I do not know the words I need to tell her.

I tell her, "I — had a stroke. — It took — my words. — hh-Wat?"

She is sympathetic but she still talks too fast. "Whatdressing? ranchbluecheese italianfrenchandthousandisland?"

I look at her bewilderingly. I need to tell her to slow down to say one salad dressing at a time. But how do I do that? I do not have the words I need. I look at Irene who says the names of the dressings for me one at a time. "Ranch?" I shake my head. And shake my head each time until she comes to "Thousand Island."

"Yes," I say and nod my head. I want Thousand Island.

Irene also takes me to the monthly women's investment club meeting. I have missed a meeting and have had a stroke in the meantime. Irene has not told anyone in the group I have had a stroke. As we meet in the parking lot there is the usual small talk as we all share what we have done since the last meeting. I am quiet, not wanting them to notice my wordlessness. Besides, I assume Irene has already told them about my stroke. Then one asked what I have been doing. "I had a stroke." They all look unbelievingly because I look normal. "It took my words." Now they are amazed. "All the words — I have, — I learned — in one month."

In the meeting, my mind races to comprehend the discussion. The financial report is particularly difficult to understand. Listening to the treasurer report does not translate into numbers for me. Even though I have a copy of the report in front of me I cannot find the numbers the treasurer is talking about. There is a new member sitting next to me. She has had a head injury and understands more than the others the trouble I am having. She leans over and points to the numbers as they are being talked about. *Ahhh,* now I understand. It is a long time before I really feel like I know what I am doing in the investment meetings again. Even then, my understanding is tempered by a very slow, muddled brain processing, and a stilted and abrupt speech pattern.

Irene walks with me along the interurban trail on the weekends, and as we walk she teaches me words. She picks a subject. For example, office words. Invoice. Memo. Credit. Bill. Payment. Register. Check. She says a word. I repeat. Then she asks me to spell it as we walk so I will be able to write the words in memos. I spell it verbally to her. She approves or corrects it. Then she goes back over the difficult ones. I like this because I am doing two things at once. I am getting my exercise and I am learning words.

From crutches to tools – letters to sounds

Irene:
You cannot drive and you, once very active, now tire quickly. That removes the small advances you made during the early hours of the day. You can say some things now in halting, basic sentences, like a person learning a second language – simple phrases adjusted to express yourself with the greatest economy of words, necessitated by the tiny vocabulary that is within your reach.

In the weeks and months that follow, you work at it constantly. I see that you realize quickly that speech therapy, the standard way of working at a return to speech, is not enough, and it is not giving you what you need. Soon, I see that you are, in fact, working out your own recovery method. I see you learn letters and their sounds, then the syllables, and the pronunciation of words. You use flashcards and we shop for books for kids learning to read. I realize that your mind is as bright, quick and efficient as ever and now very honed to the task. You know what you need, and seek out what you have figured out will work. You think over your resources and put them together, reaching out to two friends who are elementary school teachers, using the dictionary to learn to read, oxymoronic as that may sound. These words slip off my keys so easily now – no indicator of the slow, determined, difficult work this was for you.

It seems to come in piecemeal, without direction. I am always attempting to come to terms with this aching problem of having no resources. Somehow, I strongly feel letters have something to do with words, something to do with reading and writing. How do letters make words? How do letters make the words speak? As each day marches on, a day is marked against the six weeks' limit I think I have available to reach the half way point to my recovery.

An example of finding solutions by piecemeal is when Ms. Sands wants me to write sentences. They can be short. I only need three words. Sometimes I say three words that sound to me to be a sentence. I sound them out. Too many of their sounds do not produce letters that look right when I write them down. One time I need the word *so*, at least I think I do. If I can only find its spelling, I can tell. "So?" I slowly sound it out. "S" for sss, "o" for o, but there seems to me more sounds than two letters. My lips seem to end with a /w/ sound. "S-o-w." No, that does not look right.

Once at work I want to write *why* but cannot find it. I ask an employee, "How do you spell 'why'?"

"Dub el yu, a ch, wi."

Geeze, I thought I was asking for a short word, and I am given six sounds. Is that six letters? Besides, I did not recognize them.

What is so hard about *what* and many other "w" words? *What* to me sounds like it starts with an "h". "H wat." But the right side of my pictures brain does not remember having seen it spelled that way before. Does it exist? I think *what* is a short easy word. Why can I not find it? I cannot find *hwat* in the dictionary. Eventually I find that the dictionary spells it as w-h-a-t, pronounced as *hwat*.

Help comes in different forms. The *house* word is always a problem. I always want to say it *horse*. Then, Frank comes home with a Winnie the Pooh video for my amusement. (We are always grasping at straws hoping something – anything may help me.) The video opens with Pooh pictured next to his house. The narrative is moving too quickly for me to digest the story, but over Pooh's door is a hand scrawled sign: **Pooh's Howse**. *H-o-w-s-e says house. That makes sense. "Ho-w-se" is how to remember to say house.* Thereafter, each time I want to say house, I think back to Pooh's video. I picture Pooh beside his house. Then I imagine the sign over the door. I remember it is spelled h-o-w-s-e Then I am able to spit out house, not horse.

Letter names

Another time, after having worked for two hours producing a half-dozen very short sentences, I cannot spell *go*. I sense it is the word I want and that it is very short, but how to start it? It has to start with one of the letters. I go back to the letters practice columns. Yet, no letter seems to start with a /g/. Did I write them correctly in the columns on the lined yellow pad? Did I leave one out? Where can I find a list? I have already given away all the boys' children's books. We have of lot of big people books, but they are very thick and the words in them are very long and numerous. Nevertheless, I screw up my courage and look for the big red book that has lots of words in it. I do not know the name of it. Even when I look at its title, I cannot say its name. The cover is titled **Webster's New World Dictionary of the American Language**. I look at it. **Dictionary**. It will have the letters in it. Quietly, I try to say it. "Dis tī ōn ār wī." Does not seem right, but all I need right now is the letters inside. I do not see all the letters listed on one page. I use the thumb page inserts and list the letters down a piece of paper. For some reason, I notice that the "A" section starts with "A,a (ā)". That is peculiar. I did not know a letter has a pronunciation. I write down (ā) next to the "A,a". I proceed to the first entry of each letter and add each pronunciation next to its letter.

That is interesting. It is apparent that each letter has a name and a pronunciation, and its name does not necessarily start with its letter symbol. Some letter names do not have their letter symbols in them at all. For example, se for "c", je for "g", kyu for "q", dub-'l-yoo for "w", eks for "x" and wi for "y". I do notice that "f" is pronounced with a ĕf and "r" with an är. That must be why I had such a hard time learning Frank's name. When I had looked at the spelling, I tried to say the word by saying the letters. It is no wonder *Efaraenka* did not sound right, and no wonder it was difficult to remember to start it with a /f/ sound leaving out the short "e" in the front. (Slashes around a letter mark the letter as a sound.)

This exercise is not beneficial at the moment, but eventually I am able to apply it. After this, it becomes apparent that when a word is spelled to me, I can analyze it more phonetically. I learned that when someone tells me a word starts with a "wi", it is a "y", not a "w". When someone tells me I need a "dub'l-yoo", I realize they are not talking about three different letters, but a "w". The letters "g" and "j" with their "je" and "ja" sounds remain confusing.

In the meantime, I am fairly confident I do have a complete list of letters. Slowly I go over each one trying to find the one that will start my *go* word. "A. Go? No. — Be. Go? No. — Ce. Go? No. — De. Go? No. — E. Go? No. — Ef. Go? — Je. Go? — Ach. Go?" And on to the end of the letter list. Nothing wants to start with the *go* sound. Then I try again. There has to be a letter to start *go*. "K" is close, but *ko* does not look right. "Q" is close, but *qo* does not look right. I am beyond thinking and I am putting my material away to try again the next day when Tim comes home.

Consonants

"How's it going, Mom?"

"I have — to — write. — I can — not — write — the word."

"What word do you want to write?"

"Go."

"Go?"

"Go."

"Do you know the alphabet?"

"Yes!"

"Can't you go down the alphabet until you come to the one that sounds like /g/?"

"I did — that. — Nothing — says — /g/."

"Mom, 'go' is 'je-o'".

" 'Je-o'? — Write."

Tim writes "go".

"Oh, 'go'. — Tim, — 'je' — no — /g/!"

"Mom, you don't know what sounds consonants make. You need a key to show you."

"I know! — I — look-ed. — Not — here (showing him the dictionary) — or — (pointing toward the upstairs) — b - b - b-lue — books — (motioning to the many books side by side that are blue and are the **World Book Encyclopedia**)."

Tim looks around for a few minutes and says, "You're right. We'll have to make a consonant key for you. We just need an easy word that starts every consonant that you are able to remember to say. That will give you an idea of how the consonant makes its sound."

"hhWat?"

"Consonants."

Now that Tim mentions them, I know what they are. They are all the "other" letters. The big group. The ones that are not the "a, e, i, o, u" group I do not know the word for either. I ask Tim to write down *consonant* on the page I have started with the letter list. With that, I will practice saying *consonant* later. Then he thinks of easy words I will know for each consonant. He says them and I write them down with his help.

We are about half-way through the list when Tim is called to the phone. It is a long phone call, and I am unhappy with this distraction because I want to keep going. This list is an exciting breath of hope! I think this is really going to help. Helpless to dream up words myself, I need a mentor. Impatient about Tim's absence, though, I notice the dictionary still on the table. There are lots of words there! I cannot read most of them, but if I start at the beginning of each letter, I should be able to follow down the columns until I recognize a word. I could put it on the list. I start doing that while Tim is on the phone. When he is finished talking on the phone, he looks at what I am doing. I am like a school kid appreciating a teacher's attention, and I look forward to Tim helping me finish the list. But he says, "You're doing fine, Mom. I've got to run," and he leaves. But he is right; I am on the right track and I can finish the list myself. (See Appendices B, C.)

The brain that was mush before Tim came in, now buzzes with excitement. Although I am too tired to think straight, I sense this is going to be an important tool. Not only should it help me spell, but it should help me read. It should help me say words correctly. There sitting on the table is the *Reader's Digest* reminding me of the goal I had made of being able to read it before the next issue comes. That deadline is coming quickly so I vow, in spite of my weariness, to start on it before the day is over.

Using the consonant key

I take the *Reader's Digest* and the consonant key list when I go to bed. I get comfortable next to the bedside table lamp to read. My reading should not be confused with the pleasurable reading enjoyed by someone whose brain is fully intact.

This is different. This is a deliberate, slow, one piece at a time chore. Each word is dissected. Each consonant is referenced to the consonant key as I seek to find the place for it in my mouth that produces the right sound. The longer the word with more consonants, the longer the process takes. Then, if I can remember the sounds I decide are correct, I run the consonants together to see if they make a word. If I cannot remember which sounds they make, I have to start over again.

It is a mystery how I am able to hear when I have the word right. I do not know whether if it is a for-real word until I say it correctly. Somehow, it must bounce into some distant receptor in the functioning side of my brain to find recognition. And from there it comes back to me with a yes or no answer. One after the other, each word goes through the whole laborious process.

Once I have completed a sentence I am exuberant. *Oh boy, I have finished a sentence! But what about the story? What does the story say? What did it say?* More often than not, I have had to study each word with such concentration that I have not remembered the sense of them. Then I have to start over with each consonant to find the word to try to make sense of the sentence. This time I try to remember what the word means with its sounds. Once I have the sentence, I go to the next, again starting with each consonant in each word. At the end of the paragraph, I have to ask, *What has the paragraph said? Am I following the story?*

The article I am trying to read is about the Rogers family. As often as that word appears in the article, one would think that after a few times, I would remember how to say their name. This evening, I am never able to spontaneously execute the pronunciation of *Rogers*. I have *rat* as a key word for "r". Looking at it, I am reminded that "r" does not say its own name, "ar". Its sound goes along with the key word *rat*, /r/. That is fine, but there is a problem with the "g" in *Rogers*. My key does not allow for variations in the sounds of letters. My key uses *go* as a reference for the "g" sound. As hard as I try to make it sound right with my consonant key, it never seems right. It always comes out Rō-/g/-ers with a long "o" and a hard "g" as in *go*. Yet in my mind's eye, *Rogers* is a familiar word.

I develop a new crutch for bringing the Rogers' name to mind. When we were in elementary school, Mother took us to a piano teacher by the name of Mrs. Rogers. What did we call her? Each time I see that name in the article, I think about going to Mrs. Rogers' home for piano lessons. In my mind, I see her, remember her and try to remember how we said her name. *Mrs. Rogers?* I think – think – think – into the depths of bottomlessness trying to recall her name. Finally, after many minutes while an immense concentration finds no handles to grab onto, her name suddenly materializes.

"Rŏj-ers." "Rŏj-ers," I say with conviction. I will remember that. "Rŏj-ers." But alas, after a few more sentences it appears again, and I have lost it. Again, I sound out "Rō-/g/-ers." So each time it comes again I have to use the same crutches that had helped me the first time. That is many steps to produce one word. "Rŏj-ers."

It will be a long time before I learn that many consonants present different sounds. "G" is one. It is often used as /j/. For example, as /j/ in Geoff.

As tired I had been, as tired as I am, as all consuming as it is, in a couple of hours I manage to work through a few paragraphs of the *Reader's Digest*. The whole process is arduous and exhausting. Nevertheless, Tim's consonant key list helps immensely. It gives me something to hang on to. Before, it was as if I were trying to extract a car from a mud hole. The car would be mired in a slurry of mud, wheels spinning endlessly. The wheels could never find anything to grip on to. Now I have a tool that I can use to get a grip on the sounds the consonants make. It is work but it is satisfying. I go to bed with a quiet satisfaction. Contented.

The next day, my brain is in revolt. It will not look at a word all day.

A few days later, Sue Juntunen stops by the house. Sue is a special reading teacher in the Sedro-Woolley school system. She wants to hear me read.

Proudly, I pull out the *Reader's Digest* and read a passage to her. Well, I attempt to. The words do not flow. Each beginning consonant says, "Look at me. What sound do I make?" Then each consonant in the middle and the end makes the same demand. In spite of having practiced the sounding out of consonants using Tim's key, I have to think it out. I try to think quickly so the sounds will flow smoothly into words, but my tongue has a lag time response. My tongue builds the formation of each sound long after my mind directs it. My tongue trips over each part of each word. My speech sputters, stammers and has abrupt starts and stops.

Sue says I am doing well, but I will learn more quickly if I am working with less advanced material. She promises to bring me some books that will challenge me while being closer to my ability. Not long after, she drops by some third grade level books. They are all about American Indian chiefs. How does she know they will interest me? She is right; these are still a challenge.

Somewhere in the process of learning to sound words using the consonant key list, I discover the dictionary as a source for saying words even though I cannot say *dictionary*. One would think that if one cannot talk, read or write, neither can one alphabetize. But that is not the case. I can alphabetize. I can find my word in the dictionary as long as it is written out in front of me so I can repeatedly refer to the letter arrangement.

The dictionary most useful to me is the big red thick one. Eventually, I find that at the bottom of each right hand page is a summarized key to pronunciation. It shows me the pronunciation of the word I need, in much the same manner Tim's consonant list is working for me. One index finger sits on the pronunciation of the word I want, and the other index finger follows the pronunciation key at the bottom of the page. If the pronunciation shows an "a", I can look at the bottom of the page to see it makes the same sound as an "a" as in *fat*. An "ā" as the same sound as in "āpe"; "ä" as in "cär" and so forth. This is enough for most words and I use them religiously.

Spelling – finding the sounds

I show up at Julie's house for my first spelling lesson. Social niceties are brief, and we get right down to business at her dining room table. Today she is a teacher, and she has the lesson plan in place. She explains we are going to use the McCrackens' speller[6] she had used at Lowell Elementary School with her kindergarten and first grade students. In front of us is the syllabus, a much used and tattered stack of paper.

She gives me a piece of paper with lines she has drawn. The lines are spaced far apart to give me plenty of space to write on. There is a column of eight lines on the left side and a column of eight lines on the right side.

"We are going to work with 'm'", she says. "This is how it works," she draws "M m". Then she says, "Write an 'm'." Satisfied I can write an "m" she proceeds. "This is the sound an 'm' makes." She says, "/m/," with a pursed lip and asks me to repeat it. "I am going to say a word that has an 'm' at the beginning or at the end. You are going to repeat the word, and, as you say it, determine whether the 'm' starts at the beginning or at the end. Repeat it several times to feel it in your mouth as you say it. If the 'm' starts in the beginning write it down on the left line. If it is in the end, write it down on the right line."

I listen. I repeat. I write the "m" down on the left or right line depending on whether I feel it comes at the beginning or the end of the word.

Next, Julie introduces "s" and we go through the whole procedure again. Then she combines the "m" and the "s". The "f" follows. I practice "m," "s," and "f". Through the weeks new letters are added. At intervals, a short vowel is introduced. At that point, I have learned enough from the sounds of the letters introduced that I am able to spell simple words. (See Appendix D.)

In the beginning, Julie may cover two letters per lesson. It is slow because I am slow. I mean, my brain is really slow. I listen carefully with great concentration to be able to say the word after she says it, to feel it in my mouth. There is a lot of think time as I say the word and think about where it goes. Then, I have to write down the placement of the letter.

But this is going to work. We are no sooner through the letter "m"

---

6   *Spelling Through Phonics, Second Edition* by Marlene J. McCracken and Robert A. McCracken, 1996, Peguis Publishers, Winnipeg, Manitoba, Canada.

when I **know** this is going to work! I am not sure why. Julie did not tell me the title of the book is called **Spelling Through Phonics**, but phonics it is. The phonics of it is what is going to help me. Phonics make letters say words for me so I can speak.

Incidentals

Learning to read and write with its underlying phonics is vital to my speech development. But there are other aspects that contribute to my ability to make words as well. They are the little things I learn incidentally. They are things I catch-on-to or get-the-idea-of without a lot of formal instruction. Sometimes, just an idea is enough to nudge me into a new realm of discovery.

I gather flash cards hoping I will learn something from them. One deck has cards with *Big* and *Pig* printed on them. _Big_ and _Pig_? Those words sound very much the same when I say them. *What is the difference between them? Ahh, it is the _B_ and _P_.* Rolling them around in my mouth, I discover these letters are produced in the same part of my mouth. It alerts me to pay attention to letters whose sounds happen in similar places in my mouth.

Sometimes the things I learn incidentally actually come from a teacher. It will be more than three years after my stroke before I learn why I have difficulty isolating the letters for the sounds in the *m/b/p*, and *n/t/d* groups. Sue Juntunen, who is helping me with an aphasic friend, shows him he has trouble differentiating the sounds in two three-letter groups. One is m/b/p. The other is n/d/t. She explains the m/b/p letters are lip letters. The n/d/t letters are tip-of-the-tongue letters.

I look at that and think, *Darn.* I have been having trouble with the same letter groups in my spelling for three and a half years! And I learn the secret by being present when a special education teacher teaches it to another aphasic stroke victim?

I pick up prefix and suffix workbooks thinking they might help. *Re*-act, *re*-birth, *re*-cover, *re*-form. *Re*-, *re*-, *re*-, *re*-. Too many words start with *re*. No wonder I can never remember a word by only being prompted by its first sound. There are too many prefixes, and I had not been paying attention to the middle syllables. I learn to pay attention to the root word.

For a long time, I reverse compound words. *Flower-sun. Man-mail. Card-post. Watch-wrist. Chair-wheel. Fire-camp.* Why? I invert phrases, too. Why? It helps me to realize as I am listening that the last sound in a word or the last word of a phrase is the most recent in my mind. Too often, I say the last word first followed by the other(s) in reverse order. For example, *Bear Hollow* becomes *Hollow Bear.* The most recent sound landing in the brain is actually the last sound of a word or a phrase.

The last sound spoken to the brain needs to be stockpiled, and then reversed if it is to be repeated correctly. That requires a lot of mental gymnastics. With practice, I learn to recognize the words and then remember them long enough to reverse their order. I learn it is important to think first and then speak. Mentally, I attempt to construct a statement before I speak. Then, I listen to myself as I speak. Did it come out correctly? Of course, that takes time; my speech is halting with embarrassing silent spaces between phrases.

Little words are stumbling ones. As I learn to read and write, they interrupt the flow and comprehension of the material. They are the ones that say *at, in, on, off, by, up, down, inside, outside, under, over...* Eventually, I learn they are called prepositions. In this instance, I learn a lot by osmosis, absorbing their meaning and use through the material I read. Did I read it right? Did all the little words seem to make sense? I also go over and over my writing by reading aloud. I only know if the words feel right because of the examples I have read aloud.

A lot of what I learn by osmosis through reading is called grammar. No one teaches me about verb tense or sentence construction. Primarily, I mimic what I read to be able to speak.

Part Six

The Language of Numbers

A new level of exploration

The difficulties I incur with numbers are another challenge. It is a mysterious level beyond the difficulties I have with words. I assume I do not speak words simply because I do not have words in my brain. But I know numbers. I can compute with them: 1+1=2, 5-1=4, 6÷3=2, 4x4=16. I know the math of them. When I get home from the hospital, I am greeted by bank statements demanding reconciliation and piles of bills demanding payment. At the financial club meetings, most of the words revolve on numbers. As I return to work, numbers are prevalent in every aspect of retail.

It is distressing that I understand numbers yet I make mistakes saying them, make mistakes writing them down when someone is telling them to me and have no brain imagery of the numbers when they are spoken to me. Numbers, so close yet so far. So close, yet I cannot grasp them reliably when I am saying them or when I am hearing them.

Being able to cope with numbers is a long process of aimless experimentation and learning that comes with no defining lesson plan but from desperate need.

The first need presents itself the minute I get home from the hospital. It is the pile of bills and bank statements. I set the statements aside. *The bills will wait.* But bills do not wait. To pay them I need to know if we have money in the bank. Understanding the words on the bank statement reconciliation page is beyond me, yet I need to balance our account. *Where shall I start? Maybe I can copy.* I pull out the last two statements to study them to copy from them. Meaning, I study them to copy the procedure. I match critical words front to back and compare the numbers on my last statement with the ones on my check register. In comparing the numbers from the last statement, I see where the numbers had come from in the check book. The form on the back of the statement has me entering the *ending balance, additional withdrawals, additional deposits,* and the *ending (reconciled) balance.* I follow the +'s and –'s and suddenly, I have the answer. Evidently, the years I had spent reconciling with a normal brain give me some sort of a mathematical memory about handling numbers although I cannot read the instructive words on the bank statement. Not that this is done easily nor rapidly. My brain is working in ways it has not had to work before. It is always thinking with an extreme concentration.

Being able to write checks is the next need. If I can reconcile by studying old statements, I ought to be able to write checks by looking at old ones. That is if I can understand the bill. I look at a bill. I look at the total. Does the total look like it is for one month? Or did I pay the last one late, and now does it appear again making the total for two months? Does it look like it is for two months? Did I miss a month or did I make a late payment? To be sure, I look in the checkbook and old records. If I am uncertain I have Frank check it for me. In the beginning, I simply fill out the check by copying the name of the company on the *Pay-to-the-order-of* line and enter the numeric amount on the $ line. I leave the longhand written dollar amount for Frank to fill out for me. I cannot spell number words.

My inability to write out the longhand dollar amount on a check poses only one of a myriad of problems with numbers. I cannot understand numbers over the phone. I do not understand the amount given me by a clerk. At work I may give amounts incorrectly. It is all very confusing. Why is it I can recite them by rote as long as I am not thinking about them? Why do I lose them while I am reciting them? Why can I compute numbers I can look at but cannot understand the ones spoken to me? Why do I not notice if I say a number incorrectly? Is there more to numbers than I am aware of?

Obviously. Obviously, I do have problems with numbers. I do not know what their sounds say to me, and I cannot dependably say their sounds correctly. Nevertheless, the next most pressing need for me is to be able to write the spelled-out numbers on my checks. I need to do it for paying bills at home and for filling out checks for purchases at stores.

The next time I sit down to write checks, I go back to the cancelled check box. This time I look to see how I have spelled out numbers before. Slowly, I search through the old checks to find the written number to match the amount I need. It is a very slow and laborious task. Each spelled number is different and there is no order to them:

$17.00   *Seventeen and no/100*

$41.44   *Forty one and forty four/100*

$54.33   *Fifty four and thirty three/100*

$62.87   *Sixty two and eighty seven/100*

$90.11   *Ninety and eleven/100*

It does not make sense. There is no easy way to recall the spelling. It is all random. I am doing the best I can, but I am going to be a long time writing checks if I do not have a better system. Besides, I cannot take a box of cancelled checks with me everywhere I go and take the time to sort through them to find the number I need. Will it help if I memorize the spelling of each number? It cannot be that difficult. It seems to me there is a pattern about it. Once I get started, the rest should be easy.

Typically, as with my approach with letters, I make lists. As I am looking through the old checks, I am reminded that numbers have groupings so I label columns. I think I have to learn only the names of the first 10 numbers. Are there not only ten of them? I list: 1 one, 2 two, 3 three, 4 four, 5 five, 6 six, 7 seven, 8 eight, 9 nine, 10 ten. *Whoops, where did the "0" in "10" come from?* Oh, it is the first of the ten numbers; "10" is actually not one of them. Then I start the first column over again putting "0 zero" at the top of the list. Now groups of ten numbers follow nicely. Will the spellings follow as easily?

Apparently not. The spellings of the names of the numbers do not follow in a predictable pattern. There is a confusing din of sounds compared to the simplicity of the numerals.

The first number is "0" but its name *zero* never appears again. Even the *ten* numbers are not right. To follow logically, "10" should say *ten-zero,* "11" should say *ten-one,* "12" should say *ten-two* and so forth to the end of the *tens.* But instead, *ten* changes to *teen.* It is easy enough to explain that some Englishman arbitrarily added an extra "e" to that group changing *tens* to *teens* and putting it at the end to make it sound better.... but I want predictability. I look further for consistency but find only more inconsistency.

Even to say, "Ok, now we are going to change the *tens* to *teens,*" does not follow predictably. For example, "11" does not say *oneteen*. "12" does not say *twoteen*. They say *eleven* and *twelve* which do not resemble *one* and *two* or even *teen* at all! "13" does not spell *threeteen*, but *thirteen*. "15" does not spell *fiveteen*, but *fifteen*. I had never wondered why the "20's" say *twen* instead of *two*, and "30's" *thir* instead of *three*, and "40's" *for* instead of *four*, and "50's" *fif* instead of *five* – but now I do. It is very confusing to my impaired brain to be always coping with different sounds for the same number.

Looking at the *teens* however, I begin to realize why I have such a hard time writing them down when they are spoken to me. Why I have a hard time understanding numbers over the phone and when I am practicing cassette tape number drills. For example, when the speaker says "four-teen", I hear the *four* and write down "4". Then the second half of the word, *teen,* registers and I write down the "1". But "41" is not right. *Teen* goes last in the sounded out number and first in the number symbol. I must have done that automatically when I had all my brain. Somehow, I cram this new learning into a new recess in the still functioning part of my brain. Who knows where it goes or where that is? With this new reminder, my brain now races back to squeeze in the "1" in front of the "4" to show "14". It would be much easier if the *teen* sound were to come first. Teen-one, teen-two, teen-three, teen-four, teen-five, etc. to teen-nine. Not as *eleven, twelve, thirteen, fourteen, fifteen,* etc!

In further examination of the spelling number key, I also come to understand why my mistakes occur when I am writing down numbers as I am listening to them. I mix up *six* and *seven*. Both start with "s". I learn to listen for the next consonant, /x/ or /v/ sound to help me know which number it is. *Four* and *five* both start with "f" so I have to listen further to decide which one is which. When I hear *one*, I may write down "0" instead of "1". Why? In retrospect, I think my brain may have imagined *one* which starts with the letter "o" that looks the same as "0", the zero symbol. The endings *-teen* and *-ty* are very similar in sound so I have to listen for the ending /n/ sound in *-teen* to differentiate it from the ending /ē/ sound in *-ty*. (See Appendix E.)

Numbers do not say anything until they become words

Are not words *language* and numbers *math*? How can there be a *language* of *numbers*?

What should be obvious seeps in very slowly. My brain finds it more accidentally than by learning it. It should be obvious to me now that numbers have an extra dimension that letters do not have. I needed to know that numbers are symbols of mathematical measurement; letters are symbols of sound. The bridge between them, or their commonality, is when numbers become spelled out words. When they move from being a symbol of measurement to one of speech. It works both ways. Numbers do not make sounds until you spell them out. And their words do not make math until you convert them to symbols. Therein lays the language of numbers. Think about it. Try it.

Take a number, "8" for example. "8" represents : : : : (count the dots) numerical units, but it does not *say* anything. Can you find the numeral "8" in the dictionary? No, "8" is not a word. It does not *say* anything. If your brain has words to experiment with, you can find Arabic numerals in your dictionary and find "8", among others, defined as a *symbol*. "8" is a numerical symbol. In English, it is spelled and sounded from the letters e-i-g-h-t. Does "8" always say *eight*? Pick another language. Do all languages say *eight*? Spanish: *ocho*. Hungarian: *nyolc*. Italian: *otto*. No. Each language gives Arabic numerals different words – different sounds. Yet Arabic numerals, themselves, are the same from language to language.

Numeric *symbols* are distinctly different from *words*. When the speech centers of my brain functioned normally, there was an unconscious flow of information between the parts of my brain that *spoke* with words and the portions of my brain that *computed* with numbers. Now that the speech center door is locked, I use whatever open doors are available. I find myself beginning to separate numbers from their words. When computing with numbers I think and visualize their symbols. When saying numbers I think and visualize their words, their spelling.

How does it work? I do not know if whole-brained people can imagine how this happens, but perhaps the following progression will help.

Numbers: sight to sound

One night we sponsor a slide show at Base Camp. There is a raffle prize at the end of the evening. I volunteer to be the one who pulls the raffle tickets out of the hat and announce them to the audience. *Whoops, that was impulsive. I forgot I deal with numbers differently than other people. Can I make this work?* In drawing a raffle ticket, I look at the figure 00871659. It is in Arabic numbers. Arabic numbers do not *say* anything. I have to *say* something about them. To be able to say them correctly, my head races to transpose each number to letters – to words. That requires several steps more than when I had a whole brain. I hope my brain is working fast enough that my audience will not notice.

The raffle ticket begins with "00". I know I do not have to say anything for the "00" since they are in the beginning. Then I look at the remaining numbers. There are six of them. That means I could divide it into thousands. But then I would need to also say *thousand* and *hundred*. Words still come at a premium. No, that will take too many words. I decide to speak each number individually.

I see "8". I need to see its word. In my mind, I visualize the letters I had memorized from my number/word key list. "E-i-g-h-t." With that I mentally transpose the letters to phonics. Eight. *Hmmmm?* I remember from Julie's spelling lessons the "eigh" letter pattern sounds like a long "a". (All those letters just to make an "ā" sound!) Then the ending "t". /ā/ /t/. Āt. I say, "Āt."

Next I see "7". Again, my mind searches for it the way it is spelled. "S-e-v-e-n." Again I transpose it to sounds. Sĕv-en. I have to be careful. *Six* starts with an "s", too, and sometimes I confuse them. Then, when I *say* it I have to listen to myself. "Sĕv-en." Quickly, I have to make a judgment. Did I say it correctly? Did I pronounce it with a /v/ sound in the middle? Did I tack an /n/ sound on the end? Do the sounds I say match those the letters represent? If so, fine. If I say, "six", then I have to correct myself and make it plain to the audience I have made a mistake.

This repeats slowly but surely to the end of the raffle ticket number. Clearly, there is no spontaneity as I recite the numbers. There is a halting of speech as my tongue searches for the right place for the syllables. Those in the audience who know I have had an aphasic stroke hold their breath for me. Those who do not know may think I am not very smart – or perhaps I am drunk.

Numbers: sound to sight

In that example I am looking at numbers and need to be able to say them. In this example, the strategy is similar but in reverse. The numbers are given to me verbally, and I need to change them to symbols in my head so I am able to use them mathematically.

The clerk says, "That will be two eleven."

I hear *too*. *The too must be dollars*, I think. *Too? Too. Which number is it?* The *too* sound spelled that way in my head does not match a number. How many other ways can you spell *too*? *Oh, that's right. There are two more. To and two. Two matches 2. That is it. 2 dollars.*

I forget the rest, the cents part. I ask the clerk, "Two and — ?"

She says, "Two eleven."

I hear "ĭ-lev-en". *Ahh, the 'lev' part is the giveaway.* The blackboard in my mind visualizes "e-l-e-v-e-n". *Eleven, 11. That is it, $2.11.* I give the clerk two one-dollar bills, a dime and a penny.

By separating the math of numbers from the language of numbers and vice versa, I develop a fairly effective coping strategy.

At a stroke-support meeting, a speech therapist says aphasic patients need to learn math again. I want to tell her that I am one of the aphasic victims she is talking about, and that has not been my case. I know my arithmetic. I have a problem *saying* the math. How many other aphasic people have the same problem? I sense the therapist might benefit from my experience. But at the time I would have difficulty expressing it so I let it go. I suspect speech therapists can learn a lot from their patients if they ask and listen to them.

More than two years after my stroke, I attend speech at Western Washington University. A graduate student, supervised by a professor, is my therapist. One of my problems is I need to be able to write down numbers more quickly, so she drills me. As she recites numbers, I write them down. In doing that, my brain has to race to transpose the sounds of the numbers to their spellings (s-i-x, f-o-u-r, s-e-v-e-n) in my head so I can then write down their symbols (647).

We start on three and four digits and on to seven digits as in phone numbers.

Then she says, "Now we are going to work on retention of numbers."

Whoa. She does not understand my problem. She thinks I do not remember the number long enough to get it written on the paper. But the problem is I do not recognize the numbers. I explain it is not so much a matter of *retention* as it is one of *recognition*. I need to recognize the numbers first. I am not recognizing them quickly enough to write them on the page before the next batch of numbers comes. I explain I have to *hear* the numbers first. To be able to do that, I need to mentally change her spoken words to phonics and then to spelled out words (e-i-g-h-t-y, n-i-n-e). With that, I mentally match the spelled out words to numbers from the number key I have cached in my head. Then I am able to recognize the number in terms of symbols (89).

You have to be able to recognize something before you can remember it. Without recognition there is no retention.

Part Seven

Where Does Learning Go When It Can't Go Where It's Been?

Speech is the representation of the mind, and writing is the representation of speech.

—Aristotle

How does it all work?

Letters, letter names, the phonics of spelling, words, and then speech. The question remains, where does my learning go?

Stroke damaged brain matter never comes back again. Yet, relearning does find its place somewhere in the brain. Where? What part of the surviving brain matter is most likely to accept the additional learning required of speech? In a non-scientific manner, my mind ponders on the subject to be able to capitalize on my remaining strengths.

What is speech? If I evaluate speech and reduce it to its rudimentary terms, what do I get? Sound. Spacing. Measured syllables. Accent. Intonation. Rhythm. Timing. Those are also musical qualities. They seem to be intact for me, and I get meaning from a musical score. I can still carry a tune. I recognize tone and pitch. But the word part of the score? No, even though I can hum a tune, words do not come. My songs are speechless.

What else? There is a need to be able to enunciate. That means the mouth must physically make words. That is a motor skill. The rest of my body is physically coordinated. Why is it so difficult for my mouth to physically produce words?

> Each short phrase that you utter requires a specific pattern of muscular movements. The meaning of a single expression can change depending upon the degree of movement and split-second timing of scores of different muscles. "At a comfortable rate," explains speech expert Dr. William H. Perkins, "we utter about 14 sounds per second. That's twice as fast as we can control our tongue, lips, jaw or any other parts of our speech mechanism when we move them separately. But put them all together for speech and they work the way fingers of expert typists and concert pianists do. Their movements overlap in a symphony of exquisite timing."[7]

It also goes without saying that if I am to learn words and be able to speak them, I must be able to put words into my brain and have them stick. From there, I must be able to retrieve them. I miss the word bank part of my brain that saved words for me so I could retrieve them at will. What is left in my brain that might do that for me?

What is left? There is something else. It does not show itself to me in a bold declaration, but hints faintly, as an echo of words past. While it does not seem possible that this other quality in my brain can possibly help me produce words, it haunts me. It is the multitude of pictures in my mind, the memory images that at one time came with words.

The imagery of sounds

In the early stages of my stroke it is apparent to me I remember in pictures, imagery without words. I remember canoeing the Yukon River, panning for gold, forming a trucker's knot. I can draw out the floor plan of the apartment I lived in as a toddler. I can sketch the design for the next carpentry project. Yet there are no words to go with them. Sometimes I will see a "word picture" and know what it means, though I cannot say it. When I see *Frank* written out, I know it refers to my husband though I cannot say his name. I know that *McDonalds* on a sign

---

7 *Is There a Creator Who Cares About You?* Watch Tower Bible and Tract Society of Pennsylvania, Watchtower Bible and Tract Society of New York, Inc. International Bible Students Association, Brooklyn, New York, U.S.A. 1998, pg. 58. Permission granted by Watch Tower Bible and Tract Society of Pennsylvania.

below the double yellow arches is a place to buy hamburgers though I cannot say the name. I know *Haggen* is a local grocery store whose name I cannot say.

I muddle around a long time before the picture comes together. Realization comes in faint, fleeting, incomplete thoughts. It comes sporadically. Almost unconsciously.

I notice the ground under a cherry tree covered with discarded blossom parts. What are they? Thinking does not cause my mouth to spout out the word. Then somehow my mind is seeing "p-e-t-a-l-s". That is it. They are petals. The spelling comes to my head first to find the word. With the spelled image of the letters "p-e-t-a-l-s" in my head, my mouth is able to enunciate the sounds of the word.

I want to use the word *big* but the word escapes me. How to spell it? *Ahhhh, b-i-g. Big.*

I say, "Big."

After a halibut meal with Frank, Tom and Tim, I mention to them, "That was good brain food."

Brain food? Food? The word, food, is puzzling. Did I say the right word?

I ask Tim, "Food — did I — say — it right?" He said I did, but it still does not register. Faintly in my mind I am seeing "m-e-a-l" and the visualization does not seem to match the sound *food*. I ask Tim to write it for me. When he writes it on the back of the receipt, I see *food* written out. "Ahh, yes!" It took the picture of the printed out word to give meaning to me.

Eventually, I learn my greatest resource to be pictures. Pictures are the key. But how do pictures translate to speech? Are these pictures simple drawings or silent moving pictures? The limitation of using pictures as a written language tool is illustrated in the story about Sequoyah, a Cherokee Indian who was thought to have lived anywhere from 1760 to 1853.

Sequoyah observed that white people were able to communicate with "talking leaves". He wanted the Cherokee people to be able to do the same in their own language. He developed a pictograph system. For each word in his language he drew a small simplified picture. As you might imagine, it was easy for him in the beginning. A house was a house. A horse was a horse. A tree was a tree. However, the difficulty of creating simple drawings for each word started when he tried to make a house different from a home, a Paint horse different from an Appaloosa, or an oak tree different from a maple tree. The task got even more complex as he tried to further define the drawing of a man. Was he a father, a son, an uncle, a friend or an enemy?

Sequoyah accumulated so many images, he, himself, could not remember what they meant. He became so engrossed in the task he neglected his family. His angry wife burned his trunks full of word drawings. But his dream prevailed.

Finding an English spelling book offered him new hope. He could not read it, but by examining it he saw there were only 26 symbols in the book. All the words were combinations of the 26 symbols. Inspired, he started to study not the individual words his people spoke, but all the sounds they spoke. He found his language consisted of 85 or 86 sounds. By establishing a symbol (letter) for each sound in his language he found it was very easy to teach his people to read and write.

Sequoyah required an alphabet to translate *spoken* words to *written* words. I use the *written* word translated to the *spoken* word. I need to see the written word, as a word picture in my mind, to be able to retrieve the word phonetically to turn it into speech. To me, letters not only represent sounds, but they initiate the sounds I produce.

A speech clinician once challenged, "I am sure you agree that it is not necessary to read to be able to speak!" I agree that usually it is not necessary to be able to read to learn to speak. Normally, people learn to talk before they learn to read. Many remain illiterate, never learning to read at all. That is the normal progression of language among those with normal brain function. However, the aphasic does not have normal brain function. For a speech therapist to make such an assertion means they are missing a critical link between reading and speech. If speech can be symbolized in written form, why not then vice versa? Why not encourage the aphasic to use the written word to prompt speech?

My speech learning strategies are dependent on the printed words stored in my mind. From those printed images, I retrieve words. I would be helpless had I been illiterate before my stroke. Without the word echoes of the printed page still open on the right side of my brain, I would still be unable to speak.

So, where did the learning go? What part of my brain received the instructions? It went to the picture side, the printed page reading side of my brain. That is where all the new speech learning went to, and from there, it comes. Imagery of the written word is a symbol of appropriate sound. Appropriate sounds make speech.

Diagram of pathways involved with language

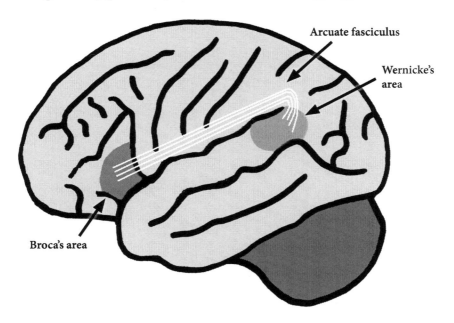

Broca's area and Wernicke's area are connected by a bundle of nerve fibers called the arcuate fasciculus.

Speaking the written word

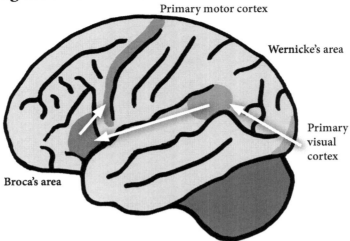

To speak a word that is read, information must first get to the primary visual cortex. From the primary visual cortex, information is transmitted to the posterior speech area, including Wernicke's area. From Wernicke's area, information travels to Broca's area, then to the Primary Motor Cortex.

Speaking the heard word

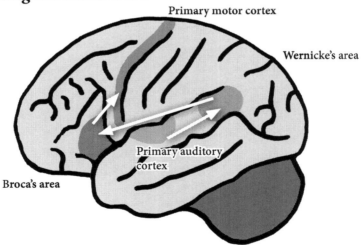

To speak a word that is heard, information must first get to the primary auditory cortex. From the primary auditory cortex, information is transmitted to the posterior speech area, including Wernicke's area. From Wernicke's area, information travels to Broca's area, then to the Primary Motor Cortex.

Neuroscience for Kids. "Oh Say Can You Say," The Brain and Language. Permission granted by Eric H. Chudler, PhD, http://faculty.washington.edu/chudler/neurok.html

Part Eight

How Long Did It Take You?

Tho' much is taken, much abides.

—Alfred, Lord Tennyson, *Ulysses*

Assumptions

There are two mistaken assumptions about brain injury recovery. One is that the damaged brain heals and function returns on its own. Thus, "It will come back." The other is that recovery has an end point. "How long did it take you?"

It was common for me to hear, "It will come back." To me, that implied there was no work entailed in recovery. No learning. However, it did not take long to discover that was wrong. Perhaps it was intended to encourage me, but …

Being optimistic, I did want to believe my speech would come back spontaneously. Each night I went to bed with faith that during the night, some miracle might mend my damaged brain. Each morning, however, as optimism turned into trepidation, my brain answered, "Sorry, nothing new since last night."

> **Irene:**
> Your speech was still very halting but I saw daily improvements in your vocabulary. Then I made a mistake – and it taught me how little I knew of what it was like to be on the inside of this. Thinking I was being encouraging when you said a word I had not heard you use since the stroke, I said, "See – it is coming back."

> You hesitated for more than the time it usually took for you to find the words and then you said, "Nothing comes back. It all has to be learned."

Yes, it took a long time for me to respond. I did not have many words then. Also, it took longer before I answered because I had to make up my mind. Were my words really coming back? Or did I consciously learn them? Learning seemed to come from so many directions. The question could be debated. But as difficult as it had been to learn words and to be able to speak them, I concluded, "Nothing comes back. It all has to be learned."

If it did not come back by itself, how long did the learning take me?

I was told by professionals that in the first six months, I would achieve 50% of the extent of my recovery. In the first year, I would reach 85%. Presumably, the last 15% would occur in the next year or so and there would be a cut-off.

Irene:
I took a trip and on the return flight, I sat beside someone who told me his wife worked as a speech therapist. I told him about you and he said it is known that any improvement in speech that can occur would occur in the first six months after the stroke. I thought of the time that had passed and the many words that were beyond your reach. I knew I was not going to repeat this to you.

I did not have words to tell Irene that my neurologist had told me that in the beginning, although I thought he said six *weeks* when he said six *months*. Those predictions hung heavy over my wordless mind. Words or no, it did not take long for me to realize that those percentages were not promises of future accomplishment relative to my pre-stroke speech competence. They were only a promise that, yes, I would have some improvement, and that improvement would occur primarily in the first year.

Potentially, there could be a large deficit between my language proficiency after my stroke and what it was beforehand. Obviously, I wanted to regain as much as possible. So the race was on, a seemingly impossible task. I was 53 years old. My language skills seemed to be three years old. How in one year could I possibly even approach what I had accomplished in the last 50 years?

How long did it take? Was there a cut-off? The following chronology shows that learning accomplishments did not come in predictable stages but in fits and starts. And they continued long past the one year limit.

First year

In the first six months from August 16, 1998 to February, 1999, life is intense. Gains are hard sought; hard found. I am hard pressed to learn words at the same time I battle a medical establishment that seems not to comprehend what it is like for me not to have words. The stroke damage in itself demands a huge amount of rest. And on top of that, I am to discover that estrogen withdrawal deprives me of sleep and causes other distressing ailments. Remedies come slowly from doctors who largely leave me on my own until I learn enough words to express my concerns.

Logically, my first step toward aphasia recovery is to take speech therapy, which I do with great enthusiasm. Surely, it will give me a firm grounding in being able to regain the language skills I have lost. In November, speech therapy ends. There is an unsettled end about it, similar to Tim's discontent in kindergarten years ago.

—∞—

Tim stood in the kitchen with me after he came home from school – full of the usual sharing about his day. Then his mood changed – different from his normal five-year-old patter.

Solemnly he said, "Mom, I'm having a terrible lifetime."

What was going on? "Why, Tim, what's the matter?"

His lower lip quivered, and his eyes began to pool. He choked up. "They're not teaching me anything in kindergarten." The tears continued down his cheeks.

—∞—

Ms. Sands gave me a 90% score saying she was sure I would be returning to work. It might well have been 90% of zero. She could not have known how empty my brain still was, how difficult it had it been for me to accomplish anything in speech and how much of it came of my own initiative.

In these first months, I keep discovering my limitations. I find learning words exhausting. The mental drain translates to a physical strain, and when I am tired, my brain revolts. I plan my schedule according to how much mental energy will be required. I schedule only one speech or spelling session in the morning because my brain will have stopped by afternoon. If I want to go to an evening meeting, I do not study words that day. When I go to work, I start late and leave early. I cannot both open and close the store the same day. The day will have been too long.

There is also a limit to how much I am able to do at work. A month after my stroke, Base Camp holds its annual Fall Sale. Usually, I will have printed and mailed the sale announcement. I will have been instrumental in determining the products for sale and marking them. On sale day, I will have been a contributing member at the pre-sale staff breakfast as we review the day's plan and divide up staff responsibilities. For this sale, my family and the staff do the preparation. I sit at the breakfast meeting with few words. I listen hard, my head bobbing back and forth from one conversation to the next, catching a word or two from one or the other, but not grasping anything. My helping has to be without words. I cannot answer the phone – cannot talk – cannot understand – or leave messages. Sometimes customers will come up with a question. Usually I cannot even understand what they were talking about. My staff tries to shield me. I help with the refreshments. Even at that, it is a chore to walk up and down the stairs. I break out in a sweat. Short of breath. Familiar faces come up to the office to say *hello* with best wishes. While faces are familiar, names evaporate. Frank takes me home mid-day to sleep.

Slowly as the weeks go by, I do make a presence at the store more often. I become the gopher. I go for office supplies, go for fast food lunches and go for building materials. That works as long as someone has prepared a list for me. Then I am able to show it to a clerk if I cannot find the item, and if I am unable to say the words myself.

Soon after the stroke I am driving again. My kids delight in sending me on errands and on this occasion send me to Hardware Sales without a list. It should not be a problem. After all, I know what I want, and I know their store almost as well as my own. As long as I do not have to say anything, life is bliss. The problem is that too many people in Bellingham recognize me but do not know I have had a stroke. In this instance, I cannot find the item I want and a clerk offers to help. I explain, "I had a stroke. — It took my words. — I do not have many words." The clerk is very patient. I am bouncing images around in my head trying to find words to go with them – rolling them around in my mouth trying to get sounds to make sense – I am stammering – speaking in an irregular, punctuated, staccato manner – not smoothly – coming slowly, very slowly.

Then one of my Base Camp customers walks by, recognizes me and notices my difficulties. He shouts out to me, "Just spit it out, come on, just spit it out!" I am the funniest thing he has seen. He laughs heartily, and passes on. I am hurt in spite of the fact that I know he may not know I had a stroke that took my words. I just have to keep telling myself, *He does not know.*

One morning, purse in hand, I am heading for the back door. One of the staff teasingly asks, "Where are you going?" I know where I am going and I know what I want. I am going to a lumber yard. I try to remember how to say the name of the store. I visualize the name of Sash and Door, but no, that was the old store. They moved and changed their name. I want to say words like, *I need another pine board for the display downstairs in the basement. I'm going down Hannegan Road to Builders Alliance to pick up one. Want me to pick up something for you?* But, no, I do not have those words. I think about what I am going to buy and how I can summarize my thoughts. I need to reduce them all to a concise idea that will accommodate my few available words. While those present smilingly wait for this to all bounce around my empty brain, I am finally able to answer, "To buy a board."

"I — had — a stroke. — It — took — my words. — I — don't — have — many — words" becomes my mantra. That introduction, a list and my stuttering and stammering speech are well received by most clerks. But one day, I drive up to the drive-through to pick up tacos for the staff. I am in line during the lunch rush, cars packed in front of me and behind me. I have memorized *twelve tacos* and have been reciting the words since I left the store. "Tw-elve ta-cos. Tw-elve ta-cos. Tw-elve ta-cos." Then, as I approach the menu board I remember I need to order drinks as well. *What are the drink words? Shoot, help!*

There is no one to help. I will have to talk to a speaker. There is no real person to show a list to. Frantically, I scan the menu board ahead of me to see if I can find the drink list. Seeing the drink icons ahead, I am able to zero in on the drink symbols when it is my turn at the speaker. I look for the Mountain Dew one and the Coke one. As best I can, I phoneti-cally sound out the names of the drinks I want from the letters. Have you ever needed to sound out *Mountain* when it appears as *Mtn*? It is a long time before I order at a drive-up again. I learned I need to go inside to the counter to talk with a real person.

I learn more by error. I cannot listen to more than one person at a time. I cannot listen to one person when there is a lot of noise going on around me. At home, I cannot study with the radio on or with the ap-pliances running. I cannot concentrate. Helping customers is difficult. If I can understand them, I do not have words to reciprocate. Promptly answering the phone is a priority at Base Camp, and I answer automat-ically only to find I cannot understand the person on the other end. I learn to say the words, "I — will — have — someone — help — you." I am the maintenance person, the carpenter, the display designer and er-rand runner.

In the first few months, I am dabbling with my speech with no assur-ance any of it will bear fruit. I go to speech therapy. I practice letters and numbers. Tim starts a consonant key for me. I make lists. I study. I read aloud. I take spelling lessons. But mostly I puzzle, wonder and ponder. With that, slowly, I unconsciously associate letters with sounds, sounds with words, and words with speech. In the end, it all coalesces into a strategy to compensate for my aphasia.

Learning is not like the old days when I had a normal brain. I do not know if it is because I do not have a teacher to lay it out for me? – To show me a plan? – To show me how all these parts would make a whole? – Or maybe it is only a matter of my dysfunctional brain. Too often I cannot remember the words I learned a minute ago, much less the day before. Learning disappears as through a sieve. There is nothing up there to contain it.

Tim and Irene are with me when I am looking for a word. They know the word I want. Tim assumes that if I just tried harder I can remember it. As if I were a child, Tim tries to coax me into remembering the word. "Come on Mom, you can do it."

But my head is empty for that word and I know it is not a case of re-membering. I am frustrated because I know Tim has my word – as if he were hiding my toy and will not give it back to me. Irene is watching, thinking it is cute to see Tim being the parent and me the child when all of a sudden I have had enough, and the roles change. I spit out demanding, "Enough! Give me the word!"

"Enough! Give me the word!" No amount of trying would have brought that word back without help. From that experience, Irene says she came to realize it was okay to help me when I am looking for a word – that my brain needs it.

Writing is an arduous task. It drains my time and physical energy. However, in December of 1998, I manage to write a letter to Dad and Aunt Helen. My father has not been well for quite some time. I want him not to worry about me and to think I am recovering from my stroke.

Reading the letter now, does not begin to suggest how difficult it was for me to write. It reads all right, though it is stilted. I made no note of how long it took me to write it, but at that stage of my aphasia it probably took several days to write that two thirds of a page. Each day I probably spent an hour or two at a time sitting at the computer thinking as hard as I could, pondering for the words I needed. My spelling was so bad the spell-checker often could not find my words. I proofed it by reading it aloud, dissecting each word phonetically and then guessing at the grammar. Did it sound right when I read it back to myself? I left letters until the next day and the next day to keep checking them. Even after I mailed one, I would wonder, *Did I say that? Was that right?* I would find mistakes many days later.

Sixth month

February 1999 is the 50% recovery mark. Frank and I have had our 30th Anniversary. Tom and Tim took us with their girlfriends to the Cliff House for dinner. Six of us at one table, and I am in the middle. In the middle and there is too much talking around the table for me to understand very much of it – though I hear it all. Frank helps me with the menu and translates for me when the waiter talks to me.

This month, I manage to call job applicants for interviews, but I construct the format and practice each spiel before I call. It is a very difficult task.

My doctor had predicted that by this time, I would be half way through of my recovery. If that is true, I am going to be severely disadvantaged. I am not speaking with spontaneity. Nor am I reading aloud with ease. I cannot read silently. In a doctor's waiting room, I look for a kid's book from the crawler's corner. The book I choose must have words a toddler might read, not the wordy elaborate story an adult might read to a child. Then I quietly mouth out the sounds of the words.

The second half of the first year is fraught with meeting life's demands with the small language resources I have acquired. I am consumed with searching, analyzing. Looking for the words I need for talking, for writing. Painfully, I read aloud continually, seeking for ways the written word will speak *to* me – speak *for* me.

March 1999 is just past the six-month 50% point. This is change-over time at the store. I am involved with changing over the basement from winter's cross-country ski equipment to summer's canoe, tent and sleeping bag equipment. I am active building and rearranging displays.

While I am present at the store more, I still do not feel comfortable helping customers. Aside from doing carpentry, I am now able to help some in the office. I can take my time there though it takes a lot of concentration. When working on a deadline, I ask Frank and his friends to leave the office. They can talk elsewhere in the store, and I cannot work in the office with their distractions. My tasks in the office, by and large, do not require speaking. Without being able to define it exactly, I am becoming visually dependent. In making inventory histories for preseason orders, I match word spelling patterns against each other. In making fax orders, I copy word group spellings and write them down. In balancing out and making deposits, I put my brain on number symbol mode and try not to think of numbers in terms of sounded out words.

In January, I had started a diary. While my entries were brief at first, they make good reminders. Quotes from my diary and letters will appear more frequently. A few examples follow.

3/3/99: My brain started clicking today. Inventorying, making orders, balances out, numbers are better.

4/26/99: Went to pick up trail passes @ Darrington ... Tom reported that Curtis Buiskool fell off a roof ...

In the spring, we are out of Forest Service Trail Passes and it will take too long to order them by mail. As the gopher, it becomes my job to drive to Darrington to purchase them. Darrington is a logging community about seventy miles from Bellingham in the foothills of the North Cascades. The drive will be a challenge for me since I have not driven there myself, and I will have to say words to people at the ranger station. To eliminate having to say too many words, I take my time in my office making out the order form ahead of time and writing out the check. Map in hand, I am able to match road signs to my destination. The drive from Bellingham to Darrington is truly beautiful. The trip feeds my soul and rewards my self-sufficiency. The real test will be whether I will be able to communicate at the ranger station. Will I be able to complete my mission without explaining, "I had a stroke. It took my words. I don't have many words." Approaching Darrington, I think about the words I will say.

"I am Carol Schultz from Base Camp in Bellingham. We need trail passes," I say as I hand the order form to the gal at the counter. By minimizing the words in my request and by not initiating small talk, I am able to leave the ranger station successfully with trail passes in hand.

When I get back to the store, I am greeted by a harried staff. Heidi had to leave work early. Her husband fell off a roof at work and hit his head. My immediate inclination is to go straight to the hospital to be with Heidi. Frank and the boys tell me, "No." The pastor has made it clear that we are not to visit. The church is taking care of everything.

The stroke did not take away my stubbornness. I want to go anyway.

The boys tell me, "Mom, absolutely not! The pastor was emphatic."

It did not set well with me. What the pastor thought may not have been what Heidi wanted. I could not believe Heidi did not want me there. When I learn Curtis' head injury is serious, and he is not expected to live, I am off to the hospital. What is Heidi's husband's name? Curt. It is Curt. All the way to the information desk. *Curt. Curt. Remember, Curt.*

To the volunteer lady, "Curt, please Curt. Curt — Bi-z-ku-l." She asks, "How is it spelled?" I do not trust myself to be able to say the letters correctly. I still have to visualize each letter's phonetic spelling to be able to say it correctly, and that sometimes takes an embarrassing length of time. I write down the name *Buiskool.* She tells me the directions.

Telling me is not enough. After eight months, I still cannot understand spoken directions. "Write, please," I motion the use of a pencil and paper. She writes down the room number, and from her pointing down the hallway in the right direction, I am fairly confident I will be able to find my way. Or, with the piece of paper in hand, someone will be able to help me.

When I find Heidi, the first thing she says is, "I'm so glad you came. I was afraid you were not coming." Sometimes a loss of words is a blessing, and in this situation I was grateful words failed. They would not have been good ones the way I felt about the way her pastor had wanted me to stay away.

In this period of time, handling the phone puts me in a state of high anxiety. In spite of that, I make more of an effort to use it. Planning what I want to say before I dial is critical. My speech is still not spontaneous. Consciously, I must use all my strategies. I must carefully listen to myself to see if I make sense. I must listen to the person on the other end of the phone more carefully – often with my brain racing to change their spoken words to spelled phonics and from that to contemporary English spelling.

For example, the caller says, "This is _ _ _ from _ _ _." I do not recognize the person's name or where he is from. Mentally translating the word sounds to phonics, the missing words are *Jorj* and *Kalafornea*. However, I do not recognize the spellings. Therefore, I do not have the words yet. The next step for me is to translate the phonic spellings into other letter combinations until they represent the sounds spelled in English. *George* and *California* look familiar. Once I *see* the words spelled out correctly in my head, I recognize the meaning of the words. Hearing them over the phone alone is not enough.

Taking messages is more of a challenge. I usually have to ask how the words are spelled, and then I have to phonetically understand which letter is being said to me. For example, if I am told the letter is "c", I must mentally visualize the "se" pronunciation spelling and match it to my memorized "letter-to-pronunciation" list to see it matches with the letter "c", not an "s". Then I can write it down. Or if they say the letter is pronounced "ach", I have to remember that sound represents the letter "h", not the letter "a". Same with phone numbers. I still have to spell the number words in my mind to visually match them to their symbolic numbers.

5/26/99: M.J. called 9:30. Dad died this morning about 10:30 Indiana. ... As much as I practice on the phone, there are some things beyond me. My father has been failing and dies. Knowing I should go home for his memorial, I wonder how I might manage the flight alone. Also, I dread how difficult it will be for me to schedule a flight over the phone. Tim, who is at the computer, says, "Mom, do you need to go to Indiana? When is the memorial?" In a few minutes he schedules a round trip flight for me. No way could I have done it myself.

5/28/99: Lv Bham 9:00 PM. Arv Ind. 8:00 AM. ... In the airport, I am reminded my speech skills are sorely lacking. This aphasia must be akin to that of a foreigner knowing very little English. After all, I am learning English as a second language – English the second time around. Announcements over the intercom are indistinct as usual, but now my aphasia does not accommodate the verbal blur. The copies of my itinerary in my pocket and purse become tattered by use as I have to open them repeatedly to see where and when I am supposed to be next. When I get to a departure desk, I find a seat in front of the desk so I can watch. I watch the reader board and the attendant. When the attendant reaches for the microphone, it is a warning for me to get ready to listen. Somehow, it helps to have warning.

6/5/99: ... J & N f/dinner ... Some people express surprise I am able to do as much as I do. Obviously, they perceive correctly I have a large deficit of words. Once I am back from Indiana we visit our friends, the Arnolds. Frank mentions I have been to Indiana.

Nancy is not sure she heard it right and asks, "Carol went to Indiana?"

"Yes," Frank replies. Nancy looks to one of us and then to the other saying to Frank, "And you flew with her?" (Her question was because she knows Frank's aversion to flying.)

"No, she flew by herself."

With a long silent pause, her jaw drops to finally say to me, "How did you do that?"

Another time, I meet a new investment club member at the library to show her how to use the Value Line Investment Survey. Helene knows me as she has been a customer for a long time, but she is new to investing. From investment club meetings she is accustomed to my slow aphasic speech that comes with a mental struggle causing long pauses at each troublesome word. As each word comes, it shoots out as a rifle bullet. Or as a marching band's cadence without predictable rhythm – with a sharp staccato attack at the start of each new found word. On this day, Helene expects me to show her where the survey is in the library, but I also want to show her how it works.

Fortunately, I do not have to retrieve too many words on my own. It is all written down in the survey. I just have to point and read aloud haltingly the printed words. I show Helene what to watch for in the charts and the places to look for the information she will need. It is a spastic presentation and my reading aloud is abrupt. Helene has been standing beside me as if she were following everything. Then I look up to see if she has questions.

Instead, the face that meets me is one of silent amazement. It is the same reaction Nancy had when she asked, "How did you do that?" So that is two people who recognize I really do have problems with speech and are surprised I am able to cope as well as I do.

At the same time, I am confronted with others who think nothing is the matter with me. Surprisingly, two are my doctors and one is my husband. They all think I am up to 90% of normal. Did I appear this dumb before my stroke?

Second year

8/16/99: Annual anniversary from the stroke & I'm still alive. Good workout … 2 dips w/poles; jog to W.F. & back; 2 dips w/poles … built up a sweat. Slight rain. … The first anniversary of my stroke passes unremarkably except I am very happy to have lived another year. I have spent a year learning my limitations, acquired some crutches to help learning words, and practiced them. I have decided to close the PFO (patent foramen ovale) in my heart and have started an exercise regimen in anticipation of having open heart surgery in October. It does not feel like my brain is done learning yet or has even reached an 85% limitation point. If there has been a decisive cut off, it is not apparent to me.

9/5/99: I went to Juntunen alone. Nice visit. Pasties. … A visit with the Juntunens is always time well spent, but to be served pasties is a special bonus! This night I enjoy their home-baked Finnish version of a

Cornish miners' meat pie and then practice words while fitting a back-pack for their daughter, Maren. I had done this at work regularly before my stroke, but coming up with technical words at this time is a challenge ... parts of the pack ... their use in relation to the body's anatomy. Words come slowly with silent spaces between them.

9/18/99: Take off for Minn ... The second time around I am able to schedule a flight myself to Minnesota to visit my friend, Jean Replinger. I stack the odds in my favor. I call the reservation desk when I am alone at home with no distractions. No radio. No dishwasher. No washing machine noise. At a time of the day when I will be alert and my brain sharp. (Well, it is all relative.) Once I am connected, I recite my special needs to the customer service person. "I had a stroke. — It took my words. — I don't have too many words. — Please talk slowly. — I may have to ask — you to say things again."

A wonderful trip to Jean's in Marshall, Minnesota. Outward Bound friends Jerry and Lynn Cox take me in for an overnight when I arrive in Minneapolis and when I depart. Then, under Jean's wing, I start an exploration of Minnesota's southwest prairie.

In a walk in Rice Marsh Park, I am struck by the wealth of bird life – and once again, by my lack of words. There is a bird very familiar to me from my Indiana childhood. It is also common to the marshes of Washington State. As well as I have known this bird, the name for it does not come spontaneously. I have to think it out. What color is it? It is black. Is it a blackbird? No. A crow? No. What is different about it? It has a colored spot on it. Ahh, red. Red black? Black red? Hmm, not enough. Where is the red? On the shoulder. The shoulder? What about that? Ahh, and in a fleeting moment *wing* flits through my mind. Then, *red winged blackbird*. Red what? What did I think? What was that? Wing. What is a wing? I mouth it out to see where it comes from in my mouth and then turn those placements phonetically to spelling. – Wa - wa - wa –. What letter starts that sound? Oh, "w"! Oh, "w-i-n-g"! Wing! Yes, the red is on the wing of the bird. No wonder it is called a Red Winged Blackbird.

Pipestone National Monument is a highlight. I had wanted to visit there since Dad told us about it when we were kids. It is not good enough to only look; I want to read every historical, archeological and interpretive word printed on every display. I quickly realize how slowly I read. Nobody stays reading at the same display nearly as long as I do. Poor

Jean patiently waits for me on a bench or rests in the car while I finish.

This trip is one of nostalgia and discovery. Somehow, the topic of my family's interest in Indian lore comes up, and I share with Jean an experience I had had with my father. I try to explain to her how being able to speak is not always necessary. The striking thing about my sharing this silent communication is that it requires speech. It is also striking that I manage to speak to her in words not used since my stroke – and that had not been used between my father and me in that experience. They materialize, albeit painfully and slowly, from nowhere.

My father was building an Indian war bonnet. He asked if I would like to help.

In relating this to Jean, finding the words I need is a challenge. *The hat part? What was it called? The bonnet or crown?* Then the next step was to describe the steps of construction. *The parts? The parts of the bird? The feather word. The bottom of the feather? The quill.* A new word.

The quill had to be prepared to accept a cord at the base.

How to describe cutting off the end? Not just to cut it off square. No, at an angle. How to say that? Sliced? Maybe. Skived? Better.

We skived the end of the quill. With that, we rolled the skived quill to make an eye at the bottom of the feather. Then we glued fluffies at the base and tip of the feather.

The type of glue we used? What was it? Dad always had an abundance of it around. We used it to fix and build anything that was small. Ahh, Duco. Duco glue. That seems right. The word list seems to go on and on. Binding. Yarn. Felt. Needle. Thread.

Maybe the reason to tell Jean the detail is to show her how many words are absent in this task of silence.

Dad and I stood side by side sharing in the construction of a complex task never saying more than a few words to each other. Although the verbal component was missing, there was a visual one. That was how we spoke to each other. I had watched Dad build a war bonnet before so I had a visual memory of how it was done. Watching each other was all the communication we needed.

Likewise, the visual components allow me to retrieve descriptive words for Jean. Each word that seems to come from nowhere comes from a painstaking search for printed words cached in my memory. Once I find the letter pattern that represents the word I want, its phonics prompt speech. More than a year after my stroke, I still have no spontaneity.

When it is time to go to the hospital for my protime, Jean insists on being with me. I assure her I will be able to manage myself. But Jean does not think my words are adequate; she wants to hover near to help me. That is okay. When I give my phone number instead of my address, Jean is at my side.

Jean suggests I write a book about my stroke recovery. That is a compliment, but at this point the idea is a far-fetched dream. Writing is a dream. I know I have made progress with language, but I cannot define the process. It will be a long time before the muddle clarifies.

9/28/99: Took Tom to his shoulder surgery. ... A new concept is presented to me while Frank and I wait for Tom's shoulder surgery. Frank reads a magazine. I cannot find one I can read easily. I am bored. I do not know how it comes to be, but Frank introduces ordinal numbers to me. First, second, third, fourth, etc. A new way to look at numbers. It is exciting to me and I want more learning, but Frank wants to get back to his magazine.

Struggle, struggle, struggle. To understand, to be understood. Happy, but everything always comes cognitively; nothing automatically. Some days my brain works cognitively and others not at all.

10/9/99: Spelling is difficult today. More than usual.

10/20/99: 5:00 AM St. Jo's ck in for PFO repair surgery. ... On this day, open heart surgery closes my patent foramen ovale (PFO), the hole in my heart that allowed a blood clot to find its way to my brain causing my stroke. With this closure, I shall be able to discontinue my Coumadin. The prospect of a blood clot reaching my brain is reduced.

11/19/99: Mary Gallagher interviewed me about stroke recovery. ... This interview for the *Bellingham Herald* is a challenge for me and for the reporter. I do not really have enough words to speak to her effectively. Neither do I really know at this time how my recovery hinges on reading. Nevertheless, Mary does a remarkable job writing the article.

My language strategies develop slowly. I practice without knowing exactly what they will do for me. I use them. I keep involved. I work. I practice writing emails to family and friends and keep a better diary.

12/17/99: While composing MJ & BA's letters found a real progress in getting the words to the page. A remarkable advancement. … It was a longer letter than I had planned, yet it seemed not to be laborious. Words seemed to just find their way to the page; mistakes easier to notice and correct. Each needed "sound" would easily finds its letter to the word. I was spending less time in the dictionary, less time bouncing around my empty brain before it would compute. And each time one of those difficulties would resolve so easily, I would feel like crying. It is clicking. Click, click, click. And every time it would click, I would again feel like crying. Why fight it, I thought? Finally in the end, I submitted. I stopped a few moments, let go, and cried. Sobbed with joy.

Finally, after 15 months, there is some sign of salvation. I am not sure what is making it work, but I am not going to argue. I rejoice.

In spite of my impairment, I am more involved with the day-to-day operation at the store. Frank is ill. Tim goes to explore Africa leaving us short on help. I hire Penny Paus. I hire Michele McFarland. Once I hire Michele, I explain to her I am aphasic, that sometimes I do not understand what is said to me, that taking messages and writing memos is a slow process for me. I may need help at the phone. She says to me, "Is that why you look at me so intently?"

2/21/00: Uneventful gathering & drive to Manning. 12 of us. … Not yet verbally qualified, but there is no one else to do it, I lead a cross-country ski vacation to Manning Park in British Columbia. Frank and I usually do it together, but he is still sick. Tim is in Africa and Tom will be needed to run the store. That leaves me.

Did Tim realize he was leaving so much work for an incompetent? Tim sends me instructions from Africa to place more preseasons. Somehow, I am also preparing the Spring Sale.

3/21/00: Have made reservations at Skamokawa Inn Paddling Center near the mouth of the Columbia. For F, BA, & Jean Aug 3, 4, 5. … Screw up my courage and get on the phone to make reservations to stay at the Skamokawa Inn Paddling Center in August. *Skamokawa* is a mouthful for a clumsy one who does not yet athletically produce words. Ska-mo-ka-wa. Seeing the word is more frightening than finally saying it. When I first came to Washington, my taxidermist employer told me that the Northwest Indian words were not too hard to say. They mostly sounded the way they were spelled.

I am starting to leave my spelling and grammar mistakes in my diary. It is encouraging when I look back on it to see some improvement. Before, I erased and wrote-over the corrections. **Now I string out my attempts at spelling and leave them.** It has occurred to me that if I am to see progress, I must see the mistakes I have made. I need to remember the agony and the reward that was in finding a word.

3/28/00: replacing the wall in the recieveing/receiving room.

Frank has me helping with canoe instruction. "Frank, what is this?"

"The thwart?"

"Ahh, yes, the throat." Realizing I have made a mistake saying the word, "No, what is it?"

"The thwart."

"The throat?"

"No, the thwart."

Shoot, how can two words sound so much alike and be so different?

Canoe instruction is fine as long as I am paddling alone with Frank in the canoe, and he is instructing. I paddle intuitively; I can demonstrate strokes without thinking. As long as I listen carefully to understand his prompts, all goes well.

Frank puts me in a canoe with one of the students. *Has he forgotten I have trouble coming up with words?* I have not practiced canoe terminology. I get in the canoe with Jason Stoane. I explain to Jason I had a stroke that cost me my words so sometimes they do not come easily. If my speech is slow, that is why. He will have to be patient with me.

163

Jason asks when my stroke was. I think it is curious he wants a specific date. Sometime later, I notice his name on one of my lab reports. A doctor, he had read my MRI at the time of my stroke. Perhaps he wanted to see it again.

4/13/00: I still have trouble picking up the lectures at the Kingdom Hall.

B-e-s-t improved. Still get my B's and F's and M's confused … An isolated line in my diary. Evidently it had taken a long time for me to decide to spell *best* starting with a "b" and not an "f" or "m".

6/6/00: Tom told me Karen Morse's husband had a left side brain stroke and I should visit them. … I do not understand what Tom said, so I ask, "Who?"

"Karen Morse," says Tom.

I think hard to make sense of it. I'm pondering, *Still not picking up names. Karen Morse? Her husband? Have I met those people?* I am still not picking up the name although Tom seems to think I should know these people. Again I ask, "Who?"

"You know, Mom," says Tom, "Karen is the president of the university."

"Oh." I have met Karen and Joe once, but they will not remember me. The prospect of encouraging the president of the university is intimidating, to say the least.

A few days later, when I gather up my courage to go to the hospital, Karen is away and Joe's brother, Fred, is with him. In meeting Fred, my confidence falters. Here is a new person with a new name I am not expecting. The difficulty I am having with his name is an example of the way my brain is still not working.

When Fred introduces himself as *Fred*, my brain does not receive it as anything I can recognize. Even after I repeat his name myself, my mind races trying to identify this word as something meaningful that I can remember. The clock is ticking and nothing is computing. I really want to remember his name. Nothing. I ask him to repeat his name again, maybe twice. Still my brain is frantically searching to find some other bit of knowledge that might match with *Fred* to make some sense of it.

At this point I realize time is running out. Fred is ready to move on, but I still do not have the information I need. I do not have his name. Finally, I ask Fred to spell his name. Even when he does, I have trouble with /f/. What letter is that? I cannot find it. I silently but visibly mouth it out – ef-ar-e-de – while he watches, and my brain keeps searching. Finally, /f/ is "f". *Fred* pops up on my mental bulletin board. *Fred* is a name I knew all the time.

"As in Frederic," I say. I have a handle on it because my neurologist is Frederic Braun. So now between Frederic Braun, and Fred Morse who is Joe's brother, I can remember *Fred*. How does it work? I am not entirely sure of the process yet. But I do know that the whole process is much more complicated to the aphasic than is apparent to the observer.

6/13/00: Took Tom to WWU for Hungary … warranties, orders, payables, desk. … The desk in the office is mine while Tom is on tour in Hungary and Italy. I enjoy being in charge making orders, entering and paying payables, processing warranties and payroll and sales tax. Most of them do not require talking. All I have to do is write things down – by looking.

6/14/00: McCrackens spelling book calls it "spelling dictation." I call it "finding the sounds."

6/19/00: … visit from Dr. Chao-Ying Wu … I have been inventory-ing in the store basement when a gentleman starts looking at paddles. I ask if I can help him. He stares at me like he knows me, and I should know him. Then he says he admitted me to the hospital for my stroke. He compliments me by saying, "You have had a remarkable recovery." I am modestly star struck. I am thinking first of all that he must have thought I didn't have much of a future when he admitted me. And sec-ondly, maybe I am making more progress than I think.

7/20/00: AM flight to Indiana. Met a woman f/Lynden on the Sea/ Chicago leg. Did talk with her about learning language/stroke as her husband is a teacher & they work with Hispanics. Flight this time much easier than last May 99. … easier to understand inter-com & reading signs. Conversation with seatmates easier.

Almost exactly two years ago, I had been paddling the Yukon River.

Now, I paddle along the Columbia River with Frank, my sister Betty Ann and my old Minnesota Outward Bound supervisor, Jean Replinger. The Skamokawa Paddling Center is our base. I am reminded that a year ago Jean suggested I write a book about my stroke. At that time, I could only dream of writing. I had not yet been able to bring words to mind, much less write them. This time, with gentle persuasion, she is more insistent. Now the possibility seems somewhat less remote. Possible? Possibly. After we part, I ponder all the way home and realize that if I am to do it, now is the time to start. It would be a long reach. Am I overly optimistic?

8/10/00: ... w/Tim to Salt Lake City. Trade show was good. I still need more words. I'm still over my head, though much easier than the shows at Seattle, and the various rep clinics in the beginner or even a year ago.

Third year

8/16/00: 2 yr stroke aniversary/anniversary - Frank now reminded my/me this am when we woke up. That then I'd been in the helicopter. Later at 10:00 that I'd been in the Fort Nelson (airport)/hospital. Here I am writing having lost the avilaty/ability then. ... That seems a long time ago, and yet, as yesterday. So much is still so fresh. So much was taken away from me. Words gone. Could not read. Could not write.

It does not seem possible I made 85% of my recovery in the first year. Certainly, I have made another 85% in the second year. My learning curve is not following the norm. Nor does it seem I am done learning. Why do they give such limits? Doctors and speech therapists probably say that because they have been told that and they do not know. They do not know from experience because they do not follow their patients long enough. It is probably all a guess, and that is too bad. Their patients believe it. Believing it, they become the casualty of a doctor induced prophecy. Given up on, they give up too soon.

And believe me, it is easy to believe time's up. Recovery is hard work. It is a convenient excuse to think it is time to give up. Fortunately or unfortunately, depending on your point of view, my learning curve continued past the first year and the second into an uneven continuum through the years. The idea that 50% of recovery will occur in the first six months and that 85% of the total will occur in the first year is extremely misleading.

> **Irene:**
> I would like to find my acquaintance of the airline flight and ask that he never again spread the misinformation that improvement is limited to what can be accomplished in the first six months.

Progress continues, and I make an effort to write more in my diary.

8/18/00: 1st day to work after the trade show and will carry journal in my purse to kep/keep at hand to make notes as strom/ke memories come back. Also am making notes where spelling is difficult. Shows language is still a problem.

8/21/00: Each visit to a doctor, I notice how easier it is to deal with appts. Understand and answer questions. Miriam [Dr. Shapiro] is devenent/deffinite/ly/definitely easier to deal with than Reilly. However, both receptionist people have slush in their mouths. Difficult to understand, my brain still works overtime to compute incoming signals.

Can hold my own at doctor's office no/now without Frank with me to interpret. Had to have Sheila or Miriam repeat themselves to me. But can understand.

Have notice I can pick up a magazine and read. 1 ½ years ago, could not read at all, or would attempt a kid's book from the crawler's corner.

8/29/00: Pleasantly surprised to see Karen Morse and Joe appear this afternoon at the store. Joe had a major leftside CVA to afect/affect/effect his right side motor skills and aphasia. He's now walking and his right arm is showing progress Karen says he's k/now at the point he wants to speak ... He's yest/just started speech therapy at St. Jo's. ... This is the first time I put words together spontaneously. When Joe walked in, I said to him, "Look at you, Joe. You are standing up on your own feet." I did not have to think up or practice in my mind the words I was going to say. They just came out on their own.

8/29/00: ... used it with a message to Barbara Smith when she'd had a heart attack in Nochia Scotia [Nova Scotia]. ... I want a special term of encouragement in a get well card for Barbara. She is a gentle, unassuming and soft-spoken neighbor down the road, and I want to find a term that will fit her well. She was one of my oldest cross-country ski students, skiing with me into her 80's. She confided that in college in Canada she played ice hockey. That is why she has false teeth behind her quiet smile. She lost the real ones to an opposition's hockey stick. Her nickname, she said, was Dirty Barb due to her ability to cuss so profoundly. "The coach required us to cuss, you know, to intimidate the competition, and I was the best." It took a long time for me to find the appropriate cliché... **Kick Butt!**

About this time I also wonder about what makes speech work and how it works for me. The results are mixed and sometimes more confusing than clarifying.

8/30/00: Speech comes from sounds and descurning/discerning sounds of the letter is not negesareily/neccesarily the same sound as that found in the word. The/an image or memory trickers/triggers meaning.

8/31/00: I notice each day how much easier the words come, how clearer my head seems to be. Answering the phone is not so much anxiety. Am reading the end of "My Year Off" by Robert McCrum and am really reading it. Last time I visited this was probably several months after my stroke and it was a proposition of one ward at a time, then make a run of it, then go a run at the sentences to make sense of the mar/paragraph.

9/2/00: In a small way, I have started documenting my stroke history. I now keep a notebook and pen in my purse. There, as thoughts come to me during the day, I jot down notes that come to my mind. Mostly just reminders; sometimes a few sentences. It's not in order; I'm just trying to prompt events so I can expand on them and make order of them later.

I am beginning to realize my brain is not really repairing itself. I am using other parts of my brain to compensate for my missing language center.

9/6/00: One thing is clear. After a stroke there is an empty space in your head, and never ever again is anything exactly the same as it was. Your brain makes new wiring, but it's hooked up in a different way that requires new methods/patterns of thinking. Your head is always compensating; it feels like there's a ball bouncing around inside your head looking for a landing spot – an answer, like it's learned. It gets easier with practice, but the ball is always bouncing … in the void.

9/9/00: Sale day. I am over my head still being on the floor. My head races to try to keep up with what the customers are saying–what they want; also with the staff. Still each time I cringe inside me after I answer the phone. Will I be able to understand what the person wants? I listen very carefully. I can't listen to another conversation. Can't have too much going on around me. Will be able I respond without my tongue tripping up in my mouth? Will I be able to "fake" it? To get by without explaining I'm aphasic?

Such benchmarks do show advancement compared to a year ago – 2 yrs ago. 2 yrs ago was 1 month from my stroke. I helped with the refreshments. I couldn't answer the phone – couldn't understand – or leave messages. Sometime a customer would come up with a ques. Usually couldn't even understand what they were talking about. It was a chore to walk up and down the stairs. I'd break a sweat. Have/be short of breath. Went home mad dy to sleep.

My year 1, could speak better – could answer phone and take mess as long as the caller was patient with me to figure out the sounding of spelling and ph numbers. Was getting up and down the stairs and good for all day. Some at register, but not in the heat of it.

Now at year 2 – sale day was exhausting tho I did remarkably better than a year ago.

9/9/00: Jennifer is getting married tomorrow. I remember the forrest/forest fire fighter f/ Cle Elum. Worked for us @ Base Camp while getting her BA in speech pathologist. Neat kid. Was going to finish a MA but was having a hard time being "in doors" for two more years so spent 3 yrs traveling, being a airline stewe/r/dess & enjoying life. Encouraged her to go back to sch for her MA & work with aphasics. That I'd coach.

9/12/00: "My Year Off" by Robert McCrum. It was given to us when I had my stroke. Frank read it first and tried to tell me about it. Shamefully I lost interest when I learned he did not really lose his words.... A fews days ago I picked it up again to finish the end of the book, and it is a beautifully crafted essay. Somehow, though, I still feel like he cheated when he wrote it. Not only was he a writer, a real writer, but he wasn't aphasic. When you're in that stage of nonfunctional-expressiveness you want to know that someone out there has come back again.

... McCrum had difficulty with enunciation, but he was not without words.

In this period of time, I am thinking seriously about the prospect of writing this book. Jean and I talk by email. She is supportive.

Jean:
Your insight and your word usage explaining the stroke must not be lost.

The insights you shared with me in the fall were very special because they were descriptions with words you found available to you from memory sustained with feeling. Therefore, they weren't the word patterns usually used to describe things. They were more colorful, more imaginary, more accurately descriptive. Because you were minus lots of words and word crutches, you used what words you could find. I heard more intuitive, descriptive and personal word pictures from you about your experience.

9/19/00: It is true, a year ago I could not write. You know it will be difficult tho not impossible to recapture the aphasia experience and the process of learning ... now. This chore is a paradox. How can you really express the experience of the absence of the spoken language when you cannot speak or write? It almost ruins the absence of language to find it again; but how else can you tell about it?

It is true that this is the time to try to remember what it was like. Each day I find more occasions like that of wanting to cry with joy ... as each time a statement rolls over my tongue unimpeded by a deliberate find of each word. I am in a time between not being able to find the words I need, and the one of almost always being able to find them. It's not easy – but manageable.

Shoot, what the heck am I thing/thinking about? Never could write in the first place! Shoot! Am I really thinking about doing this?

9/18/00: Complimented Frank on his gradual outfit (instead of causual/casual) He thought it was the funniest thing he'd heard.

9/21/00: I am more sentitive about a person's difficulty in understanding language. Today at Arby's I asked for a broccoli cheese potatoe. Only shreadded cheese (not pumped cheese), no butter. When the counter person went to the cook I could see that he (probably Hispanic) had a hard tim/time understanding the shredded vs pumped cheese. She was amused to give him the direction several times and 2 other staff members were also making facial expression to make fun of him. When the counter gal came back to me I asked if he knew English as a second language and she thought so.

I asked those present not to make fun of him and explained I'd/I was still coping with englis since a stroke 2 yrs ago. The gal says, "He can speak very easily, but he con't understand what we say." I told her it was probably he has to s/translate it into his language to make sense of it. I showed her that the cheese-shreadded was not making sense to him. He's probably not thought of it as "shredded".

9/21/00: ...sense of euphoria I felt when I realized I could now think in 1, 2 and in one, two, etc. Involved marking and sawing to length the plastic pipes. Impressed that after my stroke my head would work 74" or 37 ½" but would not work seventy four inches or thirty seven and one half inches. It's mush/much better when it does both!

9/25/00: Frank sad/said she was grabby [crabby]. In a sense I was, but mostly had to do with the aphasia. When words come at a premium you don't beat around the bush to say what you think. Get to the point without tact and when you can't find the polite word you need, a cuss word is hanier/handier.

9/30/00: Two friends of Randy – Kevin and Rock. All of them

interested in the process of stroke experience. I think Kevin asked me how it's effected/affected my brain/my mind (is he a counselor?) & I think it was Rock who/who teaches English as a second language. All suggest I write a book – first prompted by Randy. Talked with them about the relearning process & now how I think the brain goes around injured spot to compensate.

10/2/00: Irene and I have lunch and I broach with her the idea of writing this book. She says get started.

10/12/00: "H" word sill a b/problem. Have. Had. Hand. Hole (whole).

At Arby's now I can almost always understand the amount due. $1.07 now for a turnover.

Left some film off for Tom at Rite Aid. Wonderful be able to understand the directions on the envelope and almost be able to scan the page.

Thurs Night. Patagonia clinic tonight. I was very tired from weeding at store all day. Head worked more slowly, but was able to pick up more information tonight than I had previously. Still had to consentrat very carefully. Brian [the rep] noticed it and at one time asked if I had a question – just said I had to concentrate. Once or twice had him repeat for me.

10/16/00: Came home with a high tonight. Had just come from Bell/Bill Belcourt's Black Diamond clinic on skis and bindings. Tod/night I could understand the terminology, Ski, cut, sidecut, core, foam, wood, carbon fiber, shovel, waist, tail. Left, curve, tight, steep. A year ago all of this would have been a strain. As if I was floating a foot high over my head. I'd be able to snag out an isolated word hear and there and come to set in my head. But words were disjointed and made little co(h)esive meaning. 2 years ago I wouldn't even have been there. Was still so tirerd/tired out that I'd have gone home. Besides I couldn't have understood and couldn't question. Even at Xmas of 98 at Manning Park I was just then starting my ski equipment termenolgy. Ski, poles, binding, bail, boot, pins were foreign words to be relearned. Trail, trak, lodge, room. Carve, float. Floatation.

Maybe a bit leudigrust (that one was so bad it wosn't evern in the spell check and I am laughing hysterically!) Ludicrous (did I do it?)

A study suggests that cognitively learned skills are activated in one section of the brain. Then, with repetition, those skills become automatic ones in a different section of the brain. ...

10/22/00: University of Chicago Magazine October 2000 ... Chicago of University Research Imaging Center. A study about using golf swing to determine wea/whether skills are learned consciously in the brain & then move to another part of the brain that is ingrain or unconscious. I thought the study was also relevant to apraxia and aphasia.... In the beginning each sound is executed with a conscious deliberate action – to muscularly form the sound and then for the brain to consciously say the correct word. That is a visable/visible noticeable process of execution. Takes a long time, is not smooth and the "skills" are transiant/transient, temporary, elusive & require practice – repetition – constantly corrected with/whether by oneself or others. Then actions move eventual to a more smoothly, connected manner of speech with/which seems to ... become more ingrain – more natural – when words come out without thinking deliberately for each syllable, word, sequence of words ... when it seens/seems that sometimes a phrase will roll over your tongue and out your mouth as if you hadn't even been thinking. And somehow your head hears it and makes sense of it without mussing/musing over each sounds, translating it into it's spelling to run it back through re/who're/your head as a check spell? To see if you really said the right thing. Yet sometimes today the conscious process is still apparant/apparent each day.

10/24/00: I've started on the book.... I popped out a first page last night and showed it to her [Irene] today. She thinks it'll fly.... Trying to keep the sense of being aphasic after you've learned to write is very difficult.

11/6/00: Yes it is a trudge. I asked Frank if our journey had been one. It was an unequivocal, "Yes!"

11/8/00: ... to hospital to pick up 2 MRI sheets ... Jason Stoane – the hospital MD who read my MRIs ... noticed me at the imageragy (sp?) counter. Asks to see my MRI. He looked at it saying "That's a big stroke. You were lucky." I was lucky to do as well as I had? I quessin/questioned asking if it was a large stroke? He repeated it was. I mentioned my doctor told me it was a small stroke – a minor one. He said, no, mind/mine was a big one. I thanked him for his compliments as I had felt it was a "big" stroke too as hard as I had to work at it. Again he said I was lucky. He was obviously/surprised I'd improved as much as I had.

11/29/00: My head is sludge tonight.

By now, I am attempting to analyze my learning strategies. I make notes, but I am not sure my words will make sense to anyone else. Or even to me later.

When does the written word translate to the spoken word? The eye to the sound? Or visa versa?

If memory is intact, the imagery of the written word becomes a symbol of appropriate sound – to speech.

I still have a problem knowing whether the word I say is the word I mean.

12/12/00: Yesterday couldn't find "post". I was saying it but couldn't plas/place it. Had an up standing log. [Pictured in my mind]. Was saying the right thing but had to say it several times and ask Frank about it to get it to register. [To be sure what I was picturing was the same as the word I was saying.]

Found my way around word processing better today – words coming together – don't take as much pondering. The word mean something more easily.

I'm coming to a point it is hard to be detached from my stroke experience. Almost everyday the present me remembers the former self and feel emotional about it – to find it sad yet gradifying/gratifying to realize the progress I've come. If I alowed myself I would cry. Got to be detached to right/write this book.

I reach into the refrigerator – can remember when I could not say "refrigerator" – and am overwhelmed with emotion.

Tomorrow, it's make/back to the grind. ... I do it all the time. "M" and "B", and "K" and "C" still get interchanged. Aaargh!

1/10/01: Have finished pages 4 and 5. Feel my credibility disintegrating as my speech and writting ability improves.

1/22/01: The printed word became the concrete symbol in my head of the sound of the word – pinning the printed word on my memory bulletin board.

1/30/01: A discovery from the newspaper ... 26 letters and 40 sounds. That's all there is to the English language. Wish someone had told me that when it seemed impossible.

2/5/01: Did purchase a laptop thinking it would help to work on the book when I was away from home leading trips. Trouble was that Frank watches the TV in the hotel room and it is very difficult for me to concentrate and write at the same time.

Am finding a lot of subtle emotional undercurrent going on right now.

2/16/01: Every once and a while I find a few phrases rolling over my tongue out my mouth without thinking of it. Without thinking of each word, and without thinking of each word's position in my mouth ... That started last fall.

... find me trying to screw up enough courage to make another go at therapy ... ran into Carol McRandle who recommended I be evaluated at WWU [Western Washington University]...The session went well, but it had an emotional aspect I hadn't anticipated. I nearly lost it when the gals started flipping open the same spiral bound pages that Ms. Sands had used with me.... flashbacks reminded me of the helplessness I'd felt then. Then there was the catharsis of having realized some success. I could now come up with words that had not been in my head before. Amazing.

Writing proves therapeutic in that it helps my language skills. However, at the same time, it continues to bring up an emotional undercurrent.

3/8/01: She [Irene] noticed pages 6 and 7 used bigger words than the previous. It was ttre/true. It had been 2 months since I'd last worked and my vocabulary has changed. Was worried about it but thought I needed the descriptive forms to get over [portray] the feeling I had – and how my empty brain felt.

Irene likes the description on the ambulance step. I take in the day. I take in myself. She said I should ma/make note that those two short paragraphs agonized me over a 6 wk period and probably took me 8-10 hrs.

This morning I open my work and come to the 1st page. "He never turns his Flashlight ..." and sentence before "his headlamp beam focused ... reminded me how difficult it had been for me to come up with "flashlight", "headlamp" and the put [ing] [of] those sentences into sequence. I cry/cried.

... My improvement is so remarkable compared to what it had been that I am a different person–so that when I look at the former person, I cry for her. Makes writing difficult. I have to separate myself from the accomplished person as not to be subjective. Have gotten to the point I have to put myself in objective–aphasic mode to write.

3/15/01: ... closed on a condo near WWU. It has been heady stuff for me since I found it, put earnest money on it and negotiated the price while Frank was away in Salt Lake City.... Do you know how many new words there are to learn in buying real-estate when you are aphasic? Frank didn't even [mind] when he got home! Seems he trusts me more now with half a brain than he did before my stroke!

3/16/01: I find it extraordinarily difficult to write at times. Going over my notes from 6 mo ago shows so much improvement in my speaking/writing ability that I am overwelmed. Tonight was trying to write about the helicopter flight. Dug up my notes sketched back in Aug–Sept 00. I found those thought[s] simple yet profound. ... I closed my work crying. I don't think the feeling will go away as I write this book ...

A revealing article from the newspaper explains why it is difficult in English to assign letter patterns to sounds, and how to sound them out from the letters. Our alphabet has 26 letters. Our speech makes 40 sounds, and our spelling of those sounds use about 1100 combinations of letters. No wonder it has been so difficult to learn to speak when I am dependent on the visualization of letters to be able to produce sounds. It would be much easier if we had 40 letters, one per sound.

4/2/01: First speech therapy at WWU. I see nightmares of vision of small circles, large circles, small squares, and large squares. Each in four colors. Then they ask me to place the small green circle to the right of the large white square, etc. My brain balks because there is too much input. I ask to have it in smaller parts, need to say it myself. Then the professor comes in as asks me to try to do the whole think whithout asking questions without repeating the directions myself. That knocks the props out from under my compensating system. And I crash.

An observation about Joe's aphasia as I contemplate working with him, and as I also define how language now works for me. ...

4/6/01: He does better at saying the printed word than thinking it up. It seems all his words (his card words) are up in the ether. With no connection to expressiveness. Like he needs th/eathers [tethers] to bring it down to reality. He needs some anchor. Which I think is going to be the alphabet and sound pronunciation. He's missing the root of learning. 26 letters, 40 sounds of language and the combinations the 26 letters making up the 40 sounds. He's operating [asked to learn words] up in the 10's of thousands of words with no base.

As I begin to help Joe, I also investigate what other resources might be available. Over the course of the next few years, I read (after a fashion) and keep alert to any bit of information that might be beneficial.

I read *I Can't See What You're Saying* by Elizabeth Browning about her son born partially deaf with complete receptive and expressive aphasia and *A Different Drum* by Constance Carpenter Cameron who writes about her son born with absolute expressive and receptive aphasia and the methods she used to correct his impairment. In reading these books, I am struck by how there can be such a difference between a person born with aphasia and an adult like me who acquires it after years of experience with normal speech.

Into the Blue: a Father's Flight and a Daughter's Return by Susan Edsall is a particularly interesting read for me. Susan and her sister take over their father's aphasia recovery in an intensive three month period. In spite of their meeting resistance from speech therapists, they courageously develop an unconventional learning plan for their father using children's reading workbooks, among other things. It is important to note that, essentially and unwittingly, Susan and her sister provided their father with what is now considered to be the most progressive speech therapy plan available, an intensive residential aphasia program. For an example, see the University of Michigan Aphasia Program at (www.aphasiahelp.com).

A friend gives me an article: "Building a Better Brain" by Norman Doidge, MD. Doidge writes about Barbara Arrowsmith who suffered from a brain dysfunction, learned to fix her own disability, and then taught children to do the same. The implications are that an impaired brain can be trained. The article goes on, "The discovery of neuroplasticity is the continental divide of neuroscience. Before it, conventional wisdom about treating many brain problems flowed in one direction-towards compensation. But neuroplasticity challenges the idea that the only way to treat a learning disability is to 'go around' a weak area or function, and hence, never stimulate it."[8] I do not know whether my recovery is due to neuroplasticity or by "going around."

Jennifer Case, an employee, gives me one of her speech books, ***An Introduction to Language*** by Victoria Fromkin and Robert Rodman. From that, I learn about Broca and Wernicke areas of the brain. The Broca center is responsible for saying words (being expressive) and the Wernicke center allows one to understand them (being receptive). Seems like my stroke was right between those centers overlapping parts of both.

In it I also read about *voiced* sounds. That explains why I have trouble finding certain letters (spelling them correctly) when I am writing at the computer. While writing silently, no letter makes *voice* to me. I never know the difference between c, g, and k.

In ***An Introduction to Language****,* there are 40 sounds listed as "A Phonetic Alphabet for English Pronunciation." I had read about them

---

8 "Building a Better Brain" by Norman Doidge, M.D. Permission granted by Norman Doidge, www.normandoidge.com

in the newspaper, but I could not find them in the dictionary. The book uses different sound symbols for them. I make a Forty Sounds list substituting regular English alphabet letters. And, in doing so, discover some of our letters do not make sounds at all. I puzzle those out from the dictionary and add those notes myself. Well, it is not perfect, but I try. (See Appendices F, G)

Frank and I are invited to take Joe to his "head-work" session in Vancouver, British Columbia at Dr. Paul G. Swingle & Associates' office (www.drswingle.com). An associate there, Dr. Michael David de Jong (www.drmikedejong.com), works with Joe. The day we are there, a technician administers Joe's therapy and makes note of his responses. She hooks up Joe's scalp to several electrodes to measure his brainwaves. In front of a computer monitor, he watches. When his concentration in the proper brainwave is in synch, he is rewarded by a computer generated sound.

I am not sure how it can be rewarding. It sounds like a loud raucous racket to me. I am not sure how it works. It looks like voodoo to me. Nevertheless, Joe works at these sessions every week. And as I work with Joe, I see progress in his ability to concentrate, to learn. In short, it is called biofeedback. More technically, it is neurotherapy at a psychoneurophysiology clinic. I think that this therapy must work with the brain's neuroplasticity.

One of the most rewarding occasions in my search for tools and methods that might teach aphasics to speak is meeting Dr. Marsha Riddle Buly, Associate Professor in Literacy Education at the Woodring College of Education at WWU. Marsha takes me straight over to WWU's Ershig Assistive Technology Resource Center and introduces me to Linda Schleef who is coordinator and practitioner of the center. Among other aids, computer software, and electronic devices, Linda shows me WYNN™, a literacy software product, by Freedom Scientific Learning Systems Group (www.FreedomScientific.com/lsg).

It basically reads aloud to the reader. It reads any material that can be scanned. The student dictates the reading styles, size of print, line spacing, word spacing, and the rate at which the text is to be read. The student follows printed material as each word is highlighted. He can also stop at any point he wants a word repeated so he can practice how to say it. He can also click *dictionary* to see what a word means and the dictionary window talks to him, too. There are other niceties to recommend the program, but to me the biggest downfall is the level of computer literacy required to operate the software.

Would it help Joe, I wonder? Although his learning to read children's material is helping his ability to speak, he misses being able to read adult material. Whether it might help Joe, I can only guess. For one, as Linda flips from one window to another, to one toolbar to another, I have trouble following the prompts. My reading ability is still too slow. Joe's is slower than mine. Will he be able to navigate the program when he barely reads at all? Yet there are some features that would benefit Joe.

When Joe takes a look at the program, he likes it. He purchases it and finds his way around it very quickly. If you are going to have an aphasic stroke, be sure to get your Ph.D. first and know your way around a computer like Joe so you can use the WYNN™ software. Even if Joe uses it only as recreation, it still reinforces speech. The printed word pictures he needs are right there as they are being spoken.

Marsha takes me to the education section of the library and shows me the emergent reader books and then all the elementary school age books indexed by reading level. All the time I have been struggling to learn to speak, I have had no idea there is such a wonderful resource available so close to me. It would have been helpful if the speech people had referred me to the education people.

It is ironic I accumulate this knowledge after the fact. I cannot help but think it would have sped my recovery had I been taught instead of been left to discover things myself. But sometimes having worked so hard to learn something yourself is as good as or better than it might have been if it were taught.

5/7/01: ... tonight is one of those nights my head is haveing difficulty with words.

5/9/01: Speech therapy at WWU. We're working on numbers with words (feet, inches, miles, denominations, etc.) so do I catch the differences between numbers and words?

5/18/01: Dr. John Hruby stopped by to talk about his partner – Dr.

Gary Snyder who had a stroke 6 wks ago. John is really intrigued with the whole process of relearning.

I got the idea from him that doctors do assume that learning stops at 6 mo. The idea that the brain can reprogram itself past that point to compensate for the past as whel/well as absorb information beyond what one had none/known before the stroke. He seems to think it was a unique idea?!

Seems that he and Jason Stoane are intransed/intranced wh/with the similarities between my and Gary's MRI and if my learning systems might work for Gary.

5/30/01: I told Frank one of my errands was to go out to Costco … "Oh good, then get some avocados." That reminds me we also need another item. I spurt out, "And we need potato chips." As it leaves my mouth I know that is not right. I quickly say to him, "No, that's not right. It's something with a 'p' and a 't'." So I think. My head recreates the image of the thing I want. My mind flashed to the bathroom. Imagines the rolled paper beside the toilet. Searches for the spellings I need to translate it to the right sounds to get it over my tongue and out my lips. I think … p-a-p-e-r … t-o-i-l-e-t? "No. We need toilet paper. T.P." Of course, Frank is watching the wood burn within me the whole time and now laughs uproariously!" "That's a good one. I'm going to write that one down!"

6/6/01: … tried to show me how to "close-out" using the new "point of sale" computer system the kids have installed. It's going to be a push for me. The whole prompt system is dependent on written words…. I had to explain to Tim it would take a while to learn it because I will have to think about the words and their terms until they become automatic. It's not a wonder many never bother. What a slog. I hear a new career calling. It sounds like a mower cutting grass. Or cleaning homes. Sigh. Don't I wish?

My reading is getting better all the time, but it is different, and I am always working on it.

6/15/01: The big thing of me today was this morning when I bought donuts @ the Red Apple. This time, when Adeline said the price [was] six eighty five my mind "knew" it was right when I heard it.

I entered the amount on the card swiper <u>before</u> it occurred to me I should check the amount on the monitor. Bingo. It was right – for the first time, I knew it would be right.

7/13/01: In Minneapolis waiting for a plane to Indianapolis. I am definitely having problem understanding over the intercom–the breakfast options, flight #s, time, directions to gates, etc.

8/9/01: Aunt Helen is comatose this morning. MJ & Bruce followed the ambulance ...then MJ, BA, I & Frank went back to hospital for a song fest. AH in much better shape. Still on IV & O_2. ... We are attending the Hipple family reunion at Lake Tahoe, California. During this reunion, our Aunt Helen becomes very ill and is taken to the hospital. There, in her room, my sisters and I sing Girl Scout songs to her. It is now three years since I lost my words and my singing words would not keep up with the music. This time, as long as I am following printed words, I am sometimes able to keep up. When it gets too hectic, I hum.

Fourth year and counting

On August 16, 2001, it has been three years since my stroke. All in all, life is good. My PFO is closed. I am off Coumadin. I sense the uphill battle is nearly over, and I am looking forward to enjoying good health again. Before my stroke, I had imagined each birthday to be the halfway point of my life. Now I am feeling that way again. I count my blessings and am appreciative that my remaining brain cells are compensating for me.

Another anniversary and am I done? Is this how long it took me to recover? I speak well enough that many have forgotten I lost my words. Seemingly, the fundamental compensatory strategies I will need throughout my aphasic lifetime are in place, and the whole process of having acquired this degree of language proficiency is promising. As a matter of fact, it is even comforting! However, years will be needed before they become predictable and definable tools ... until they become ingrained – automatic.

As the years pass, I write in my diaries less about my stroke recovery and more about everyday events. Still, once in a while, it is apparent my mind is still improving:

5/6/05: Remarkable since about November, I've noticed that I can read much more easily. I guess reading feels more comfortable and the prospect of wading through a pile of "foreign" material is not as threatening it had been. Still I compensate in many ways that others don't notice. I still struggle comprehending numbers and words given me orally over the phone. Even if a word is spelled out aloud for me, I sometimes do not understand the letters being given. Also, I still do a poor job in comprehending numerical data given orally and knowing what it says. I need to see it written down. Likewise, I am apt to say numbers incorrectly.

In so many ways I am still tied to being able to translate sounds—whether it be numbers or words—into the image of their spelling. Always now I work by imagery, imagery on the other side of my brain.

That applies specifically to my reading ability, but my speech has also followed a similar course. It shows that my mind is still cognitively processing language, but at the same time it is doing it more rapidly. As a matter of fact, my strategies work well enough that their many cognitive steps appear to come automatically. A friend observes, "That is interesting. No one would know that sometimes you struggle."

Could there be any higher praise? Nor could there be a better time for me to say, "That is how long it took!"

Glossary

Acute hemorrhage   Severe hemorrhage

AFIB   Atrial Fibrillation

Alcan   Alaska-Canada Highway

Antiaggragants   Antiplatelets

Anticoagulant   A substance that delays or counteracts blood coagulation. That is, it stops blood from clotting.

Antiphospholipid syndrome (APS or APLS) or **antiphospholipid antibody syndrome**   A disorder of coagulation, which causes blood clots (thrombosis) in both arteries and veins.

Antiplatelet agents   Drugs that interfere with the blood's ability to clot.

Antonyms   A word that means the opposite of another word.

Aphasia   Without speech. A loss of the power to use or understand words as the result of brain damage caused by stroke, injury or birth defect.

Apraxic speech   The inability to perform complex movements in speech, often as a result of brain damage, e.g. following a stroke.

Atrial   Relating to the upper chambers of the heart.

Atrial fibrillation   An irregularity in the rhythm of the heartbeat (arrhythmia) caused by involuntary contractions of small areas of heart-wall muscle. Familiarly called atrial fib.

Autoimmune   The failure of an organism to recognize its own constituent parts as self which results in an immune response against its own cells and tissues.

BCP   Birth Control Pills

Bifurcations   Divided; to be split or branched off into two parts, or split something into two parts.

Birth control pills (BCP)   Oral contraceptives, sometimes also used in hormone replacement therapy.

Broca's aphasia   A condition characterized by either partial or total loss of the ability to express oneself, either through speech or writing.

Cardiogenic embolism   A blood vessel obstruction resulting from activity or disease of the heart.

Carotid   A large artery on each side of the neck that supplies blood to the brain.

Cerebral artery   An artery is a blood vessel. Cerebral is relating to or involving the brain or any part of it. Relating to or located in the front part of the brain.

Cerebral Ischemic Attack (CIA)   Where the brain or parts of the brain do not receive enough blood flow to maintain normal neurological function.

Cerebrovascular disease   Relating to or involving the blood vessels that supply the brain.

Cerebrovascular Accident (CVA)   A stroke. The death of brain tissue resulting from lack of blood flow and insufficient oxygen to the brain.

CIA   Cerebral Ischemic Attack

Clot   As in blood, a thick mass of coagulated blood.

Computed Tomography (CT)   A technique for producing x-ray images of cross-sections of the body.

Cortex   The outer covering of the brain.

Coumadin   A prescription blood-thinning drug used to treat or prevent blood clots.

CT   Computed Tomography

CVA   Cerebrovascular Accident

Deep Venous Thrombosis (DVT)   Formation of a blood clot, or thrombus, inside a blood vessel.

Digraphs   A pair of letters that represents a single speech sound.

Diphthongs   A complex vowel sound in which the first vowel gradually moves toward a second vowel so that both vowels form one syllable.

Doppler ultrasound   An ultrasound-based diagnostic imaging technique used to visualize subcutaneous body structures including tendons, muscles, joints, vessels and internal organs for possible pathology or lesions.

DVT   Deep Vein Thrombosis

Dyspnea   Difficulty in breathing, often caused by heart or lung disease.

Echocardiogram   Known as a cardiac ultrasound, it uses standard ultrasound techniques to image two-dimensional slices of the heart. The latest ultrasound systems now employ 3D real-time imaging.

Edema   A general term for the accumulation of excess fluid in any body tissue, cavity, or organ, except bone.

EKG   Electrocardiography

Electrocardiography (EKG)   A procedure by which a physician obtains a tracing of the electrical activity of the heart.

Embolism   Obstruction of a blood vessel by an embolus, or blood clot, that has been transported by the circulatory system.

ER   Emergency Room

Ergot – Fungus derivatives used in medicine.

Etiology   The set of factors that contributes to the occurrence of a disease.

Expressive aphasia   Difficulty in speaking and writing. Also known as Broca's aphasia; comes from damage to Broca's area in the frontal lobe.

Estrogen   A steroid hormone produced mainly in the ovaries.

Follitropin   Follicle-stimulating hormone

FSH – Follicle-stimulating hormone

GYN   Gynecologist. A physician who specializes in medical and surgical care to women.

Helo   Helicopter

Hematologist   A medical specialist who treats diseases and disorders of the blood and blood-forming organs.

Hemodynamically   The study of the forces involved in the circulation of blood.

Hemorrhage   Intracerebral hemorrhage; bleeding in the brain caused by the rupture of a blood vessel within the head; the escape of blood from the vessels.

Heparin   A drug used to treat and prevent blood clots in the veins and arteries.

Hormone Replacement Therapy (HRT)   Medical treatment that relieves symptoms experienced by some women during and after menopause.

HRT   Hormone Replacement Therapy

Hyperphospholipid   An excessive phospholipid condition.

Hypertension   A condition in which constricted arterial blood vessels increase the resistance to blood flow.

Infarct   An area of tissue that has recently died as a result of the sudden loss of its blood supply, e.g. following blockage of an artery by a blood clot.

INR   International Normalized Ratio

Insomnia   Condition in which a person has difficulty getting sufficient sleep.

Insular cortex   A cerebral cortex structure deep within the lateral sulcus between the temporal lobe and the parietal lobe. The overlying cortical areas are the opercula (meaning "lids") and these are formed from parts of the enclosing frontal, temporal and parietal lobes.

International Normalized Ratio (INR)   Measurement used to monitor the effectiveness of blood thinning drugs such as warfarin.

Ischemia   An inadequate supply of blood to a part of the body, caused by partial or total blockage of an artery.

IV   Intravenous

Intravenous (IV)   Medical injection of a therapeutic liquid directly into somebody's vein. Also, the equipment used to administer an IV.

Left temporal lobe cortex   Located to the side of and below the lateral sulcus, a part of the cortex related to the understanding of language, or Wernicke's center.

Lupus anticoagulant   An antibody to phospholipids in a cell that can cause clotting of blood in arteries and veins and lead to embolisms, heart attacks, strokes, and spontaneous abortion.

Magnetic Resonance Imaging (MRI)   An imaging technique that uses a large circular magnet and radio waves to generate signals from atoms in the body. These signals are used to construct images of internal structures.

Medevac   Medical evacuation of injured to the nearest hospital or place of treatment by helicopter or airplane.

Medroxyprogesterone   A synthetic progestin used in combination with hormone replacement therapy.

Middle cerebral artery   One of the vessels that conveys blood from the heart to the tissues of the brain.

Migraine   Severe headache that is typically confined to only one side of the head.

MRI   Magnetic Resonance Imaging

Naturopathic   A system of medicine founded on the belief that diet, mental state, exercise, breathing, and other natural factors are central to the origin and treatment of disease.

Neurology   The branch of medicine that deals with the structure and function of the nervous system and the treatment of the diseases and disorders that affect it.

Occupational Therapy (OT)   Rehabilitative therapy that uses the activities of everyday living to help people with physical or mental disabilities achieve maximum functioning and independence at home and in the workplace.

OP   Surgical Operation

Opercular cortex   Pertaining to an operculum (a lid or covering structure), and cortex (external layer of the cerebellum).

OT   Occupational Therapy

Oxygenated   To be combined with oxygen.

Palpitations   Unusual heart activity.

Paradoxical stroke   An infarct with no obvious cause.

Patent Foramen Ovale (PFO)   A defect in the septum (wall) between the two upper (atrial) chambers of the heart.

PFO   Patent Foramen Ovale

Phlebitis   Thrombophlebitis, inflammation of the veins marked by pain and swelling.

Phonics   A method of teaching reading in which people learn to associate letters with the speech sounds they represent, rather than learning to recognize the whole word as a unit.

Phospholipids   A phosphorus-containing lipid found in double-layered cell membranes.

Physical Therapy (PT)   A physical procedures used in the treatment of patients with a disability, disease, or injury to achieve and maintain functional rehabilitation and to prevent malfunction or deformity.

Placenta   A vascular organ that develops inside the uterus of most pregnant mammals to supply food and oxygen to the fetus through the umbilical cord.

Platelets   Tiny colorless disk-shaped particles found in large quantities in the blood that play an important part in the clotting process.

Popliteal   A vein relating to or located in the part of the leg behind the knee joint.

Posterior middle cerebral artery   One of the vessels that conveys blood from the heart to the tissues of the brain.

Prefix   A linguistic element that is not an independent word, but is attached to the beginning of a word to modify its meaning.

Progesterone   A sex hormone produced in women.

Prothrombin time (PT), prothrombin ratio (PR) and **international normalized ratio (INR)**   Measures of the extrinsic pathway of coagulation.

Protime   The prothrombin time.

Provera   A synthetic hormone replacement therapy drug.

Proximal lesser saphenous   **Proximal:** nearer to the point of reference or to the center of the body than something else is. **Lesser saphenous:** either of two major veins in the leg that run from the foot to the thigh near the surface of the skin.

PT   Physical Therapy. Also, Protime.

Pulmonary specialist   Specialist who is relating to or affecting the lungs.

Receptive aphasia   An inability to comprehend spoken language. Also known as Wernicke's aphasia. It comes from injury to the Wernicke's area in the left temporal lobe.

Rheumatologist   A specialization in rheumatic diseases marked by painful inflammation of the connective tissue structures of the body.

Rhymes   A word with an ending that sounds similar to the ending of another word.

RIND   Reversible Ischemic Neurological Deficit

Stenoses   A constriction or narrowing of a duct, passage, or opening in the body

Subacute   Not as abrupt as in the acute form and with symptoms less severe and of shorter duration than chronic.

Superficial   Relating to, affecting, or located on or near the surface of something.

Synonyms   A word that means the same, or almost the same, as another word in the same language, either in all of its uses or in a specific context.

TEE   Transesophageal Echocardiogram

Telemetry   Use of electrical or electronic equipment for detecting, collecting, and processing physical data of one form or another at a given site, and then relaying this data to a receiving station at another site where the data can be recorded and analyzed.

Temporal cortex   In reference to the temporal lobe of the brain which is part of each side or hemisphere of the brain that is on the side of the head, nearest the ears. The comprehension of language is dependent upon Wernicke's area of the temporal lobe in the brain

Thrombosis Formation of a blood clot, or thrombus, inside a blood vessel.

Thrombo embolic A clot that breaks free and travels to a different part of the circulatory system.

Thrombolysis The breaking down of a blood clot by infusion of an enzyme into the blood.

Thrombus A blood clot that forms in a blood vessel and remains at the site of formation.

TIA Transient Ischemic Attack

Transcatheter A fine tube inserted into the body to introduce or remove fluids.

Transient Ischemic Attack (TIA) A ministroke, temporary and reversible.

Transesophageal Echocardiogram (TEE) A diagnostic test using an ultrasound device that is passed into the esophagus of the patient to create a clear image of the heart muscle and other parts of the heart.

Valsalva maneuver Increasing of pressure in the thoracic cavity. The action of attempting to breathe out against a closed glottis, which increases pressure in the thoracic cavity and hinders the return of venous blood to the heart.

Vasculitides The plural of the word vasculitis, which may be used to describe any disorder characterized by inflammation of the blood or lymph vessels.

Warfarin A prescription blood-thinning drug used to treat or prevent blood clots. Classified as an anticoagulant.

Wernicke's aphasia A condition characterized by either partial or total loss of the ability to understand what is being said or read.

X-rays Penetrating electromagnetic radiation, having a shorter wavelength than light.

Appendix A

Insights for Advocates

Although needs vary among aphasic people, these points may be beneficial as you relate with them. In wanting to help aphasics, you do not want to demand too much, but neither do you want to give up on them too soon.

▶ After a stroke, aphasic victims will usually retain their memory and intelligence. The challenge is being able to understand what is going on behind their wordlessness. Not only do you wonder what is going on in there and what will be the end result, but they do, too.

▶ Watch, observe, and reinforce any positive progress to help them capitalize on their remaining mental assets.

▶ Remember that the learning process after a stroke does not have a time limit or a stopping point.

▶ It is never too late to benefit from effective speech therapy. Some aphasics are able to successfully resume speech therapy several years after initial attempts have failed.

▶ Allow aphasics to be slow. An impaired brain works like an outmoded computer with some of its chips missing. You waited on your old computer. Give aphasic people the same consideration. The gift of time is the most important contribution you can give to the brain-impaired.

▶ Speak clearly and enunciate precisely.

▶ Use simple words.

▶ Speak to them slowly, as, for example, with the tempo of a waltz compared with that of a polka. This gives their brain time to digest your words.

► Make short statements without convoluted sentences. Pause at the end of each **short** phrase to let that sink in. Do the same thing when giving choices. Otherwise they will still be puzzling out the first part of the statement when the next barrage of sentences comes in. For example: "Are you cold?" Wait until they respond. Then ask, "Do you want a blanket?"

► Try to involve them with decision making. Allow them to express opinions.

► Do not leave the observer wondering about the peculiar mannerisms of an aphasic person. It is alright to say, "This is George. He had a stroke that affects his speech." It fosters understanding, acceptance and improved communication.

► Recognizing personal and place names may be difficult for aphasics. It may help to make cross references for them if a word is not computing. If they did not recognize *Gary*, they might understand *your brother Gary in Idaho*. *The Columbia* might not register, but *the Columbia River* might.

► Understanding what aphasics are saying is a challenge. Sometimes a "20 Questions" approach will help to narrow down the unknown. Sometimes a paper and pencil will help. Have them draw pictures. Sometimes they can write out key letters of the word they want to say. Use maps. That can help narrow down "place". You may have to teach them gestures, and then remind them to use them.

► Depending on the injury, aphasics may not know whether the words they speak make sense or not. Sometimes they are sure what they said was correct, and they expect you to understand. They may also expect you to make it right for them. Be considerate when they make mistakes by asking if they *meant to say ...* or did they *really mean ...* without contradicting them with an argument.

► Newly learned words do not necessarily find a permanent place in the aphasic brain right away. Help them re-learn what they learned yesterday – or even a few minutes ago – with gentle repetition. *You* are the one with a normal brain. Use a little ingenuity and creativity to find ways to help them remember.

► Involvement with social activities is important. Keeping them in the mainstream will keep familiar words before them, and that will foster speech.

► Uselessness is the kiss of death. As soon as possible, help them find purpose and accomplishment if they are not doing that already.

► Be sensitive to the fact that very few aphasic stroke victims will ever have a complete recovery in spite of the fact they may look and sound quite normal.

Appendix B

Tim's Consonant Key

VOWEL			ALPHABET CONSONANT
A	Aa	(ā)	
	Bb	(bē)	BIG
	Cc	(sē)	(S) CEILING CHOC/CHAIR (K) CAROL
	Dd	(dē)	
E	Ee	(ē)	
	Ff	(ĕf)	FRANK FLAME
	Gg	(jē)	GO GOOD GREEN GLORY GIVE
	Hh	(āch)	HI HELLO HELP HAY HEY HAPPY HARD
I	Ii	(ī)	
	Jj	(jā)	JAW JUST JOB JESUS JAM
	Kk	(kā)	KAY HELP KEEP KING
	Ll	(ĕl)	LOOK LEAP LOVE LIKE LEARN
	Mm	(ĕm)	MOM MADAME MOOSE
	Nn	(ĕn)	NAME NECK NOOSE
O	Oo	(ō)	
	Pp	(pē)	PENNY PIN PANCAKE PEN POT PIG
	Qq	(kyōo)	QU QUESTION QWEST
	Rr	(är)	READ RIP IRONIC RAY RABBIT
	Ss	(ĕs)	SAY SPELLING SEE SOB
	Tt	(tē)	TIM TUB TRY TAP THE THREE
U	Uu	(yōo)	ULTRA UMBRELLA UP UGLY URE UNBEND URN
	Vv	(vē)	ALL VOWELS
	Ww	(dŭb'əl-yōo)	WE WHEEL WHEAT WRAP WYATT
	Xx	(ĕks)	ZĂN ZĔN ZÏR ZĪ ZĬ
	Yy	(wī)	YUU + ALL MOST VOWELS
	Zz	(zē)	VOWELS + ZY (zi) ZW

197

Appendix C

Tim's Consonant Sound Key Summarized

A a . . . . (ā)
B b . . . . (bē) . . . . big
C c . . . . (sē) . . . . Carol
D d . . . . (dē) . . . . Dad
E d . . . . (ē)
F f . . . . (ĕf) . . . . Frank
G g . . . . (jē) . . . . go
H h . . . . (āch) . . . . Hi
I i . . . . (ī)
J j . . . . (jā) . . . . jam
K k . . . . (kā) . . . . king
L l . . . . (ĕl) . . . . love
M m . . . . (ĕm) . . . . Mom
N n . . . . (ĕn) . . . . name
O o . . . . (ō)
P p . . . . (pē) . . . . pig
Q q . . . . (kyū) . . . . quack
R r . . . . (är) . . . . rat
S s . . . . (ĕs) . . . . see
T t . . . . (tē) . . . . Tom
U u . . . . (ū)
V v . . . . (vē) . . . . van
W w . . . . . . (dŭb ′ĕl-yoo) . . . . we
X x . . . . (ĕks) . . . . x-ray
Y y . . . . (wī) . . . . you
Z z . . . . (zē) . . . . zebra

Appendix D

McCrackens' *Spelling Through Phonics* – Sample Work

In this exercise, after introducing a letter, the teacher says a word with the letter coming at the beginning or end of the word. The student listens and repeats the word. The student writes the letter on the left or right line depending on whether they felt it came at the beginning or the end of the word.

Introducing *M*

Monster	M	
Tram		M
Milwaukee	M	
Million	M	
Chum		M
Minimum	M	M
Macadam	M	M

Introducing *S*

Sam	S	
Seven	S	
Atlas		S
Bus		S
Support	S	
Sis	S	S
Sweets	S	S

Practicing *M* and *S*

Stem	S	M
Mass	M	S
Storm	S	M
Mounts	M	S
Stream	S	M
Scream	S	M
Sports	S	S

Introducing *F*

Frontier	F	
Frown	F	
Calf		F
Cliff		F
Father	F	
Reef		F
Fling	F	

Practicing *M*, *S*, and *F*

Floss	F	S
Form	F	M
Muss	M	S
Molasses	M	S
Self	S	F
Mischief	M	F
Stuffs	S	S
Flaps	F	S

Spelling words after adding *B*, *T*, *C*, and short *a*

tab	bat	mat	am	fat
mast	fact	fast	Sam	tact
at	cats	tam	cat	sat
cast	masts	stab	tabs	aft
Mac	act	stabs	mats	

Spelling Through Phonics, Second Edition by Marlene J. McCracken and Robert A. McCracken, 1996, Peguis Publishers, Winnipeg, Manitoba, Canada.

Appendix E

The Language of Numbers Key

0 _zero_	10 ten	20 twenty	30 thirty	40 forty
1 one	11 eleven	21 twenty-one	31 thirty-one	41 forty-one
2 two	12 twelve	22 twenty-two	32 thirty-two	42 forty-two
3 three	13 thirteen	23 twenty-three	33 thirty-three	43 forty-three
4 four	14 fourteen	24 twenty-four	34 thirty-four	44 forty-four
5 five	15 fifteen	25 twenty-five	35 thirty-five	45 forty-five
6 six	16 sixteen	26 twenty-six	36 thirty-six	46 forty-six
7 seven	17 seventeen	27 twenty-seven	37 thirty-seven	47 forty-seven
8 eight	18 eighteen	28 twenty-eight	38 thirty-eight	48 forty-eight
9 nine	19 nineteen	29 twenty-nine	39 thirty-nine	49 forty-nine

50 fifty	60 sixty	70 seventy	80 eighty	90 ninety
51 fifty-one	61 sixty-one	71 seventy-one	81 eighty-one	91 ninety-one
52 fifty-two	62 sixty-two	72 seventy-two	82 eighty-two	92 ninety-two
53 fifty-three	63 sixty-three	73 seventy-three	83 eighty-three	93 ninety-three
54 fifty-four	64 sixty-four	74 seventy-four	84 eighty-four	94 ninety-four
55 fifty-five	65 sixty-five	75 seventy-five	85 eighty-five	95 ninety-five
56 fifty-six	66 sixty-six	76 seventy-six	86 eighty-six	96 ninety-six
57 fifty-seven	67 sixty-seven	77 seventy-seven	87 eighty-seven	97 ninety-seven
58 fifty-eight	68 sixty-eight	78 seventy-eight	88 eighty-eight	98 ninety-eight
59 fifty-nine	69 sixty-nine	79 seventy-nine	89 eighty-nine	99 ninety-nine

100 one hundred	1,000 one thousand
1,000,000 one million	1,000,000,000 one billion

Appendix F

Finding the Forty Sounds

Consonants:

1.	p	pill
2.	b	bill
3.	m	mill
4.	f	feel
5.	v	veal
6.	t	till
7.	th	thigh
8.	*th*	*th*y
9.	d	dill
10.	n	nil
11.	s	seal
12.	sh	shill
13.	z	zeal
14.	zh	azure
15.	ch	chill
16.	j	Jill
17.	k	kill
18.	g	gill
19.	h	heal
20.	l	leaf
21.	r	reef
22.	y	you
23.	w	witch
24.	wh	which
25.	ng	ring

Vowels:

26.	a	bat
27.	a	bait
28.	a	sofa
29.	a	bar/pot
30.	e	beet
31.	e	bet
32.	i	bite
33.	i	bit
34.	o	boat
35.	o	bore
36.	oo	boot
37.	oo	foot
38.	oi	boy
39.	ou	bout
40.	u	butt

Appendix G

Working with Forty Sounds

Consonants:

	Symbol/Name	Key Word
1.	p (pe)	pat
2.	b (be)	bat
3.	m (em)	mat
4.	f (ef)	fat
5.	v (ve)	vat
6.	t (te)	tat
7.	th	thin
8.	*th*	*th*e
9.	d (de)	dad
10.	n (en)	need
11.	s (es)	sat
12.	sh	shop
13.	z (ze)	zero
14.	zh	azure
15.	**ch** (t+sh)	chocolate
16.	j (ja)	jam (d+zh)
17.	k (ka)	Karen
18.	**g** (je)	go
19.	h (ach)	hat
20.	l (el)	love
21.	r (ar)	rat
22.	y (wi)	you
23.	w (dub'l u)	water
24.	wh (hw)	what
25.	ng	sing

Vowels:

	Symbol/Name	Key Word
26.	a	apple
27.	a (a)	bacon
28.	*a*	sofa
29.	a	car
30.	e (e)	beet
31.	e	bed
32.	i (i)	bike
33.	i	hit
34.	o (o)	boat
35.	o	fork
36.	oo	boot
37.	oo	foot
38.	oi	boy
39.	ou	out
40.	u	up

The missing letters:

c (se)	= **k** as in <u>c</u>at	(**k**at)
	= **s** as in <u>c</u>elery	(**s**el' er i)
	= **ch** (t+sh) as in <u>c</u>ello	(**ch**el' o)
q (ku)	= **k** as in <u>q</u>uick	(**k**wik)
x (eks)	= **zi** as in <u>x</u>ylophone	(**zi**' lo fon)
	= **ks** as in fo<u>x</u>	(fo**ks**)

Common variations of *ch, g*:

ch	= **ch** (t+sh) as in <u>ch</u>ocolate	(**ch**ok' o lat)
	= **sh** as in <u>ch</u>ampagne	(**sh**am pan')
	= **k** as in <u>ch</u>emistry	(**k**em' is tri)
g	= **j** as in Geoff	(**J**ef)

Appendix H

Information Contacts*

Aphasia
www.emedicine.com/neuro/topic437.htm

Aphasia Hope Foundation
www.aphasiahope.org
Tel: 913-484-8302

American Heart Association
www.heart.org
Tel: 888-4STROKE (888-478-7653)

American Heart Association
Stroke Connection Magazine
www.strokeassociation.org
Tel: 888-4STROKE (888-478-7653)

American Speech-Language-Hearing Association
www.asha.org
Tel: 800-638-8255

Harvard Brain Tissue Resource Center (Brain Bank)
www.brainbank.mclean.org
Tel: 1-800-BrainBank

Journal of Stroke and Cerebrovascular Diseases
www.strokejournal.org

National Aphasia Association
www.aphasia.org
Tel: 800-922-4NAA (4622)

*URL addresses current as of publication date, July 2010.

National Institute on Deafness and Other Communication Disorders
National Institute of Health
www.nidcd.nih.gov
Tel: 800-241-1044

National Institute of Neurological Disorders and Stroke
National Institute of Health
www.ninds.nih.gov
Tel: 800-352-9424

National Stroke Association
www.stroke.org
Tel: 800-STROKES (800-787-6537)

Neuroscience for Kids – Language
http://faculty.washington.edu/chudler/lang.html

SAFE – Stroke Awareness for Everyone
www.strokesafe.org

The Stroke Network
www.strokenetwork.org

University of Michigan Center for the Development of Language and
    Literacy
Residential Aphasia Program
http://www.med.umich.edu/opm/newspage/2003/aphasia.htm

Acknowledgements

The prospect of writing a first book is a daunting proposition for anyone. But for me, without a fully functioning brain language center, it has been a formidable challenge. It could not have been done without the help of the many who contributed to its completion.

Jean Replinger, a longtime friend, was the first to suggest I write my story. At the time, I could barely speak, much less write. Later she broached the subject again saying it was time to start. Thank you, Jean, for initiating the process and for so kindly pushing me along.

Irene Rinn, my good friend and self-appointed editor, has encouraged me, sustained my efforts and promoted the cause since day one, page one. Words do not begin to express my appreciation of you, Irene. So, as in the beginning when words were scarce, I offer a measured, deliberate, "Thank – you." You are going to be such a good professional editor.

Molly McKitterick (thewordprocess.com) said when we met, "… it is very difficult to imagine one's mind without words – much less describe it using words. But we are going to do it." If she had second thoughts about editing this book, she got over them quickly once she wrapped her accomplished mind around my impaired one. Thoughtful and tactful, her excellent recommendations greatly improved the final read. Thank you, Molly, for your professional book doctoring.

Kate Weisel (weiselcreative.com) formatted the manuscript and designed the cover. A skilled technician with an artistic bent, her extraordinary creativity has been invaluable. Thank you, Kate. Working with you has been a joy.

Tom Schultz, my son and personal IT person, fixed my computer when it crashed and kept its memory banks open. Thank you, Tom. Having kids is such a blessing!

Frank, my husband, kept the home fires burning while I was consumed by writing. Thank you, Pard, for your support, and for being the final arbiter of any compositional decision.

For friends and family not mentioned here by name, please accept my sincere *thank you* for your personal interest in the formation of this book and for encouraging its completion. It has been a grand adventure.

About the Author

The author was raised in Boy Scout Camp Bradford, a 1200 acre woods near Martinsville, Indiana with her two sisters. She graduated from Indiana University, Bloomington with a BS in Recreation and Outdoor Education. She held various positions in youth camps and the Minnesota Outward Bound School. She has been an outdoor education teacher, a taxidermist's helper, a district executive with the Girl Scouts of America, a cross-country ski and canoe instructor and a merchant. She and her husband, with their two sons, operated their family owned specialty sporting goods store, Base Camp, in Bellingham, Washington for 31 years until their retirement.

Settled into their log home by a gurgling creek, the author and her husband are enjoying retirement the way most people do ... the fun things like taking road trips and building and fixing ... the mundane things like falling trees, piling brush, stacking firewood and digging in the garden ... and the meaningful things like being a Grandma and Grandpa helping their grandchildren explore the out-of-doors by taking them hiking, cross-country skiing and canoeing.

Made in the USA
Charleston, SC
26 March 2011